BRITISH POETS SERIES

William Shakespeare: *Selected Sonnets and Verse*
edited, with an introduction by Mark Tuley

Edmund Spenser: *Poems*
selected and introduced by Teresa Page

Robert Herrick: *Selected Poems*
edited and introduced by M.K. Pace

John Donne: *Poems*
selected and introduced by A.H. Ninham

D.H. Lawrence: *Selected Poems*
edited with an introduction by Margaret Elvy

Percy Bysshe Shelley: *Poems*
selected and introduced by Charlotte Greene

Sir Thomas Wyatt: *Love For Love: Selected Poems*
edited by Louise Cooper

Thomas Hardy: *Selected Poems*
edited, with an introduction by A.H. Ninham

Emily Brontë: *Poems*
selected and introduced by Teresa Page

John Keats: *Selected Poems*
edited with an introduction by Miriam Chalk

Henry Vaughan: *Poems*
selected and introduced by A.H. Ninham

The Crescent Moon Book of Love Poetry
edited by Louise Cooper

The Crescent Moon Book of Nature Poetry From Langland to Lawrence
edited by Margaret Elvy

The Crescent Moon Book of Metaphysical Poetry
edited and introduced by Charlotte Greene

The Crescent Moon Book of Elizabethan Love Poetry
edited and introduced by Carol Appleby

The Crescent Moon Book of Romantic Poetry
edited and introduced by L.M. Poole

Blinded By Her Light The Love-Poetry of Robert Graves
by Jeremy Robinson

The Best of Peter Redgrove's Poetry: The Book of Wonders
by Peter Redgrove, edited and introduced by Jeremy Robinson

Peter Redgrove: Here Comes the Flood
by Jeremy Robinson

Sex-Magic-Poetry-Cornwall: A Flood of Poems
by Peter Redgrove, edited with an essay by Jeremy Robinson

Brigitte's Blue Heart
by Jeremy Reed

Claudia Schiffer's Red Shoes
by Jeremy Reed

By-Blows: Uncollected Poems
by D.J. Enright

Shakespeare: Love, Poetry and Magic
in Shakespeare's Sonnets and Plays
by B.D. Barnacle

The Crescent Moon Book of
Mystical Poetry In English

The Crescent Moon Book of
Mystical Poetry In English

Edited by Carol Appleby

CRESCENT MOON

Crescent Moon Publishing
P.O. Box 1312
Maidstone, Kent
ME14 5XU, U.K.
www.crmoon.com

First published 1994. Second edition 2008 . Revised 2016.
Introduction © Carol Appleby, 1994, 2008, 2016.

Printed and bound in the U.S.A.
Set in Garamond Book 12 on 15pt.
Designed by Radiance Graphics.

British Library Cataloguing in Publication data

Appleby, Carol
The Crescent Moon Book of Mystical Poetry in English. –
(British Poets Series)
1. Christian poetry, English 2. Mysticism – Poetry
I. Appleby, Carol II. Book of Mystical Poetry in English
II. Mystical Poetry in English
821'1.0080382

ISBN-13 9781861711342
ISBN-13 9781861715289

Contents

ANONYMOUS
(13th century)

"Of one that is so fair and bright"

OF ONE that is so fair and bright,
Velut maris stella,
Brighter than the dayes light,
Parens et puella,
I cry to thee; thou see to me!
Lady, pray thy son for me,
Tam pia,
That I mote come to thee
Maria.

Lady, flower of alle thing,
Rosa sine spina,
Thou bore Jesu, heavenes king,
Gratia divina,
Of alle thou nearst the prize,
Lady, queen of Paradise
Electa.
Maide mile mother is
Effecta.

Of care conseil thou art best,
Felix fecundata,
Of alle weary thou art rest,
Mater honorata.
Beseech him with milde mood
That for us alle shed his blood
In cruce
That we moten come to him
In luce.

All this world were forlore
            Eva peccatrice,
Till our Loverd was y-bore
            De te genetrice.
With *'Ave'* it went away
Thuster night, and com'th the day
            Salutis.
The welle springeth out of thee
            Virtutis.

Well he wot he is thy son
            Ventre quem portasti;
He will not werne thee thy bon,
            Parvaum quem lactasti.
So hende and so good he is,
He haveth brought us to bliss
            Superni,
That hath y-dit the foule pit
            Inferni.

ANONYMOUS

(13th century)

"Love me brought"

LOVE ME brought,
And love me wrought,
    Man, to be thy fere.
Love me fed,
And love me led
    And love me lettet here.

Love me slew,
And love me drew,
    And love me laid on bier.
Love is my peace;
For love I chese,
    Man to buyen dear.

Ne dread thee nought,
I have thee sought,
    Bothen day and night,
To haven thee
Well is me,
    I have won in fight.

RICHARD ROLLE
(1290-1349)

Love Is Life

LIF IS lif that lasteth ay, ther it in Crist is fest,
When wele no wo it chaunge may, as written hath men wisest;
The night is turned into day, the travail into rest.
If thou wil love as I thee say, thou may be with the best.

Love is thought with gret desire of a fair loving;
Love is likened to a fire that quenchen may no thing;
Love us clenseth of our sin, love our bot shal bring;
Love the Kinges hert may win, love of joy may sing.

The sete of love is set ful hegh, for into heven it ran;
Me think that it in erth is slegh, that maketh man pale and wan;
The bed of blisse it gase ful nigh – I tel thee as I can;
Though us think the way be dregh, love coupleth God and man.

Love is hotter than the cole; love may non beswike;
The flaume of love who might it thole if it were ever y-like?
Love us covereth and maketh in quert and lifteth to heven- rike;
Love ravisheth Crist into our hert – I wot no lust it like.

Let to love, if thou wil live when thou shal hethen fare.
Al my thought to Him thou yive that may it kepe fro care.
Loke thy hert fro Him not twin, though thou in wandring ware;
So thou may Him weld with win, and love Him evermare.

Jesu, that me lif hath lent, into thy love my bring;
Tak to thee al myn entent, that thou be my desiring.
Wo fro me away wer went and comen my coveiting,
If that my soul had herd and hent the song of thy praising.

Thy love is ever-lastand fro that we may it fele;
Therin me make brenand that no thing may me kele.
My thought take in thy hand and stabil it every dele,
That I be not heldand tolove this worldes wele.

If I love an eartly thing that payeth to my will,
And set my joy and my liking whenit may cum me till,
I may me drede of deperting, that wil be hote and ill;
For al my welth is but weeping when pine my soul shal spill.

The joy that men hath sene is liekened to the hay,
That now is fair and grene and now waiting away.
Such is this world, I wene, and shal be to domes day
In travail and in tene, for flee no man it may.

If thou love in al thy thought, and hate the filth of sin,
And gif my hert Him that it brought, that He it weld with win,
As thy soul Crist hath sought and therof wold not blin,
So thou shal to blisse be brought and heven won within.

The kind of love this es, ther it is trusty and trew:
To stand in stablenes and chaunge for no new.
The lif that love might find, or ever in hert it knew –
Fro care turneth that kind, and led in mirth and glew.

For-thy love thou, I rede, Crist, as I thee tele.
With aungels take thy stede; that joy looke thou not selle.
In erthe thou hate no quede but that thy love might felle;
For love is stalwarth as dede, love is hard as helle.

Love is a light birthine, love gladdeth yonge and olde;
Love is withouten pine, as lovers han me tolde;
Love is a gostly wine that maketh bigge and bolde;
Of love no thing shal tine that it in hert wil holde.

Love is the swetest thing that man in erth hath tone;
Love is Goddes derling, love bindeth blood and bone.
In love be our living – I wot no better wone;
For me and my loving love maketh both be one.

But fleshly love shal fare as foth the flowr in may,
And lasting be no mare than it wer but a day;
And soroweth sethen ful sare her proudehede and her play,
When they been casten in car til pine that lasteth ay.

When erth and air shal been, then may they quake and drede,
And up shal rise al men to answer for her dede.
If they been seen in sin, as now her lif they lede,
They shal sit hel within, and derkness have to mede.

Rich men her hand shal wring and wicked werkes bye;
In flaume of fire knight and king with sorow and shame shal lye.
If thou wil love, thenmay thou sing to Crist in melodye;
The love of Him overcometh al thing, in love we live and dye.

ANONYMOUS

(14th century)

from *The Cloud of Unknowing*

BUT NOW thou askest me and sayest, 'How shall I think on Himself, and what is He? and to this I cannot answer thee but thus: 'I wot not.'

For thou hast brought me with thy question into that same darkness, and into that same cloud of unknowing, that I would thou wert in thyself. For of all other creatures and their works, yea, and of the works of God's self, may a man through grace have full head of knowing, and well he can think of them: but of God Himself can no man think. And therefore I would leave all that thing that I can think, and choose to my love that thing that I cannot think. For why; He may well be loved, but not thought. By love may He be gotten and holden; but by thought never. And therefore, although it be good sometime to think of the kindness and the worthiness of God in special, and although it be a light and a part of contemplation: nevertheless yet in this work it shall be cast down and covered with a cloud of forgetting. And thou shalt step above it stalwarthy, but listily, with a devout and a pleasing stirring of love, and try for to pierce that darkness above thee. And smite upon that thick cloud of unknowing with a sharp dart of longing love; and go not thence for thing that befalleth.

ANONYMOUS
(15th century)

"Quia Amore Langueo"

IN THE vale of restless mind
 I sought in mountain and in mead,
Trusting a true love for to find,
 Upon an hill then took I heed;
 A voice I heard – and near I yede –
  In huge dolòur complaining tho:
 'See, dear soul, my sidès bleed,
  Quia amore langueo.'

Under this mount I found a tree;
 Under this tree a man sitting;
From head to foot wounded was he,
 His hartè-blood I saw bleeding;
 A seemly man to be a king
  A gracious face to look unto.
 I asked him how he had paining.
  He said: *Quia amore langueo.*

'I am true love that false was never:
 My sister, man's soul, I loved her thus;
Because I would on no wise dissever,
 I left my kingdom glorious;
 I purveyed her a place full precious;
  She flit, I followed; I loved her so
 that I suffered these painès piteous,
  Quia amore langueo.

'My fair love and my spousè bright,
 I saved her from beating and she hath me bet;
I clothed her in grace and heavenly light,
 This bloody surcote she hath on me set.
 For longing love I will not let;

Sweetè strokès by these, lo!
　I have loved her ever as I het,
　　Quia amore langueo.

'I crowned her with bliss, and she me with thorn;
　I led her to chamber, and she me to die;
I brought her to worship, and she me to scorn;
　I did her reverence, and she me villainy.
　To love that loveth is no maistry;
　　Her hate made never my love her foe;
　Ask then no mo questions why,
　　Quia amore langueo.

'Look unto mine handès, man!
　These gloves were given me when I her sought;
They be not white, but red and wan,
　Embroidered with blood, my spouse them bought;
　They will not off, I leave them nought,
　　I woo her with them wherever she go;
　These hands full friendly for her fought,
　　Quia amore langueo.

'Marvel not, man, though I sit still;
　My love hath shod me wonder strait;
She buckled my feet, as was her will,
　With sharpe nails - well thou maist wait!
　In my love was never deceit,
　　For all my members I have opened her to;
　My body I made her heartès bait,
　　Quia amore langueo.

'In my side I have made her a nest;
　Look befalle how wide a wound is here!
This her chamber, here shall she rest,
　That she and I may sleep in fere.
　Here may she wash, if any filth were,
　　Here is succour for all her woe;
　Come if she will, she shall have cheer,
　　Quia amore langueo.

✧ *19*

'I will abide till she be ready,
  I will her sue if she say nay;
If she be reckèless, I will be ready,
    If she be dangerous, I will her pray.
    If she do weep, then bid I nay;
        Mine arms be spread to clip her me to;
    Cry onès: I come. Now, soul, assay!
        Quia amore langueo.

'I sit on an hill for to see far,
  I look to the vale; my spouse I see:
Now runs she awayward, now comes she nearer,
    Yet fro my eye-sight she may her flee;
        I run tofore to chastise her foe.
    Recover, my soul, again to me,
        Quia amore langueo.

'My sweetè spouse, will we go play?
  Apples be ripe in my gardène;
I shall clothe thee in new array,
    Thy meat shall be milk, honey, and wine.
    Now, dear soul, let us go dine,
        Thy sustenance is in my scrippè, lo!
    Tarry not now, fair spousè mine,
        Quia amore langueo.

'If thou be foul, I shall make thee clean;
  If thou be sick, I shall thee heal,
If thou aught mourn, I shall bemene.
    Spouse, why wilt thou nought with me deal?
    Thou foundest never love so real;
        What wilt thou, soul, that I shall do?
    I may of unkindness thee appeal,
        Quia amore langueo.

'What shall I do now with my spouse?
  Abide I will her gentleness.
Would she look onès out of her house
    Of fleshly affections and uncleanness,
    Her bed is made, her bolster is bliss,
        Her chamber is chosen, such are no mo.

Look out at the windows of kindness,
Quia amore langueo.

'Long and love thou never so high,
    Yet is my love more than thine may be;
Thou gladdest, thou weepest, I sit thee by;
    Yet might thou, spouse, look onès at me!
    Spouse, should I alway feedè thee
        With childès meat? Nay, love, not so!
    I prove thy love with adversity,
    Quia amore langueo.

'My spouse is in chamber, hold your peace;
    Make no noise, but let sleep.
My babe shall suffer no disease,
    I may not hear my dear child weep;
    For with my pap I shall her keep.
        No wonder though I tend her to:
    This hole in my side had never been so deep,
    Quia amore langueo.

'Wax not weary, mine own dear wife:
    What meed is aye to live in comfort?
For in tribulation I run more rife
    Oftentimes than in disport;
    In wealth, in woe, ever I support,
        then, dear soul, go never me fro!
    Thy meed is markèd, when thou art mort,
    Quia amore langueo.

WALTER HILTON

(c. 1340-1396)

from *The Ladder of Perfection*

YOUR SOUL is a spiritual mirror in which you may see the likeness of God. First, then, find your mirror, and keep it bright and clean from the corruption of the flesh and worldly vanity. Hold it well up above the earth so that you can see it, and our Lord reflected in it. In this life all chosen souls direct their effort and intention to this end although they may not be fully conscious of it. It is for this reason, as I said earlier, that at the beginning and early stages of their spiritual life many souls enjoy great fervour and sweetness of devotion, and seem all afire with love; but this is not the perfect love or spiritual knowledge of God. You can be certain that however intense the fervour felt by a soul – even if it is so intense that the body appears unable to bear it or melts into tears – so long as its conception and experience of God is largely or wholly dependent on imagination rather than on knowledge, it has not yet attained perfect love or contemplation.

JULIAN OF NORWICH
(1342-after 1429)

from *Revelations of Divine Love*

I SAW that He is to us everything that is good and comfortable for us: He is our clothing that for love wrappeth us, claspeth us, and all encloseth us for tender love, that He may never leave us; being to us all-thing that is good, as to mine understanding.

Also in this he shewed a little thing, the quantity of an hazel-nut, in the palm of my hand; and it was as round as a ball. I looked thereupon with eye of my understanding, and thought: What may this be? And it was answered generally thus: It is all that is made. I marvelled how it might last, for methought it might suddenly have fallen to naught for little[ness]. And I was answered in my under-standing: It lasteth, and ever shall [last] for that God loveth it. And so All-thing hath the Being by the love of God.

In this Little Thing I saw three properties. The first is that God made it, the second that God loveth it, the third that God keepeth it. But what is to me verily the Maker, the Keeper, and the Lover – I cannot tell; for till I am Substantially oned to Him, I may never have full rest nor very bliss: that is to say, till I be so fastened to Him, that there is right nought that is made betwixt my God and me.

WILLIAM SHAKESPEARE
(1564-1616)

"Now the hungry lion roars"

NOW THE hungry lion roars,
And the wolf behowls the moon;
Whilst the heavy ploughman snores,
All with the weary task fordone.
Now the wasted brands do glow,
Whilst the screech-owl, screeching loud,
Puts the wretch that lies in woe
In remembrance of a shroud.
Now it is the time of night
That the graves, all gaping wide,
Every one lets forth his sprite,
In the church-way paths to glide.
And we fairies, that do run
By the triple Hecate's team
From the presence of the sun,
Following darkness like a dream,
Now are frolic.

Puck. *A Midsummer Night's Dream*, 5.1.360-376

"Ye elves of hills, brooks, standing lakes, and groves"

YE ELVES of hills, brooks, standing lakes, and groves;
And ye that on the sands with printless foot
Do chase the ebbing Neptune, and do fly him
When he comes back; you demi-puppets that
By moonshine do the green sour ringlets make,
Whereof the ewe not bites; and you whose pastime
Is to make midnight mushrooms, that rejoice
To hear the solemn curfew; by whose aid –
Weak masters though ye be – I have bedimm'd
The noontide sun, call'd forth the mutinous winds,
And 'twixt the green sea and the azur'd vault
Set roaring war. To the dread rattling thunder
Have I given fire, and rifted Jove's stout oak
With his own bolt; the strong-bas'd promontory
Have I made shake, and by the spurs pluck'd up
The pine and cedar. Graves at my command
Have wak'd their sleepers, op'd, and let 'em forth,
By my so potent art. But this rough magic
I here abjure; and, when I have requir'd
Some heavenly music – which even now I do –
To work mine end upon their senses that
This airy charm is for, I'll break my staff,
Bury it certain fathoms in the earth,
And deeper than did ever plummet sound
I'll drown my book.

Prospero. *The Tempest*, 5.1.33-57

JOHN DONNE
(1573-1631)

Upon the Annunciation and Passion
Falling Upon One Day, 1608

TAMELY, FRAIL body' abstain today; today
My soul eats twice, Christ hither and away.
She sees him man, so like God made in this,
That of them both a circle emblem is,
Whose first and last concur; this doubtful day
Of feast or fast, Christ came, and went away;
She sees him nothing twice at once, who is all;
She sees a cedar plant itself, and fall,
Her maker put to making, and the head
Of life, at once, not yet alive, and dead;
She sees at once the virgin mother stay
Reclused at home, public at Golgotha.
Sad and rejoiced she 's seen at once, and seen
At almost fifty, and at scarce fifteen.
At once a son is promised her, and gone,
Gabriel gives Christ to her, he her to John;
Not fully a mother, she's in orbity,
At once receiver and the legacy;
All this, and all between, this day hath shown,
Th' abridgement of Christ's story, which makes one
(As in plain maps, the furthest west is east)
Of the angels' *Ave*, 'and *Consummatum est.*
How well the Church, God's court of faculties
Deals, in some times, and seldom joining these;
As by the self-fixed pole we never do
Direct our course, but the next star thereto,
Which shows where the'other is, and which we say
(Because it strays not far) doth never stray;
So God by his church, nearest to him, we know,
And stand firm, if we by her motion go;
His Spirit, as his fiery pillar doth

Lead, and his church, as cloud; to one end both:
This Church, by letting these days join, hath shown
Death and conception in mankind is one.
Or 'twas in him the same humility,
That he would be a man, and leave to be:
Or as creation he had made, as God,
With the last judgement, but one period,
His imitating spouse would join in one
Manhood's extremes: he shall come, he is gone:
Or as though one blood drop, which thence did fall,
Accepted, would have served, he yet shed all;
So though the least of his pains, deeds, or words,
Would busy a life, she all this day affords;
This treasure then, in gross, my soul unplay,
And in my life retail it every day.

Ascension

SALUTE THE **last and everlasting day,**
Joy at the uprising of this sun, and son,
Ye whose just tears, or tribulation
Have purely washed, or burnt your drossy clay;
Behold the highest, parting hence away,
Lightens the dark clouds, which he treads upon,
Nor doth he by ascending, show alone,
But first he, and he first enters the way.
O strong ram, which hast battered heaven for me,
Mild lamb, which with thy blood, hast marked the path;
Bright torch, which shin'st, that I the way may see,
Oh, with thine own blood quench thine own just wrath,
And if thy holy Spirit, my Muse did raise,
Deign at my hands this crown of prayer and praise.

from *Divine Meditations*

1

I AM a little world made cunningly
Of elements, and an angelic sprite,
But black sin hath betrayed to endless night
My world's both parts, and, oh, both parts must die.
You which beyond that heaven which was most high
Have found new spheres, and of new lands can write,
Pour news seas in mine eyes, that so I might
Drown my world with my weeping earnestly,
Or wish it if it must be drowned no more:
But oh it must be burnt; alas the fire
Of lust and envy have burnt it heretofore,
And made it fouler; let their flames retire,
And burn me O Lord, with a fiery zeal
Of thee and thy house, which doth in eating heal.

7

AT THE round earth's imagined corners, blow
Your trumpets, angels, and arise, arise
From death, you numberless infinities
Of souls, and to your scattered bodies go,
All whom the flood did, and fire shall o'erthrow,
All whom war, earth, age, agues, tyrannies,
Despair, law, chance, hath slain, and you whose eyes,
Shall behold God, and never taste death's woe.
But let them sleep, Lord, and me mourn a space,
For, if above all these, my sins abound,
'Tis late to ask abundance of thy grace,
When we are there' here on this lowly ground,
Teach me how to repent; for that's as good
As if thou hadst sealed my pardon, with thy blood.

from *Holy Sonnets*

V

I AM a little world made cunningly
Of Elements, and an Angelike spright,
But black sinne hath betraid to endlesse night
My worlds both parts, and (oh) both parts must die.
You which beyond that heaven which was most high
Have found new sphears, and of new lands can write,
Powre new seas in mine eyes, that so I might
Drowne my world with my weeping earnestly,
Or wash it, if it must be drown'd no more:
But oh it must be burnt! alas the fire
Of lust and envie have burnt it heretofore,
And made it fouler; Let their flames retire,
And burne me ô Lord, with a fiery zeale
Of thee and thy house, which doth in eating heale.

ROBERT HERRICK
(1591-1674)

To Meddowes

YE HAVE been fresh and green,
    Ye have been fill'd with flower:
And ye the Walks have been
    Where Maids have spent their houres.

You have beheld, how they
    With *Wicker Arks* did come
To kisse, and beare away
    The richer Couslips home.

Y'ave heard them sweetly sing,
    And seen them in a Round:
Each Virgin, like a Spring,
    With Hony-succles crown'd.

But now, we see, none here,
    Whose silv'rie feet did tread,
And with dishevell'd Haire,
    Adorn'd this smoother mead.

Like Unthrifts, having spent,
    Your stock, and needy grown,
Y'are left here to lament
    Your poore estates, alone.

Eternitie

O YEARS! and Age! Farewell:
      Behold I go,
      Where I do know
Infinitie to dwell.

And these mine eyes shall see
      All times, how they
      Are lost i'th'Sea
Of vast Eternitie.

Where never Moone shall sway
      The Starres; but she,
      And Night, shall be
Drown'd in one endlesse Day.

GEORGE HERBERT
(1593-1632)

The Starre

BRIGHT SPARK, shot from a brighter place,
    Where beams surround my Saviours face,
        Canst thou be any where
          So well as there?

Yet, if thou wilt from thence depart,
    Take a bad lodging in my heart;
        For thou canst make a debter,
          And make it better.

First with thy fire-work burn to dust
    Folly, and worse then folly, lust:
        Then with thy light refine,
          And make it shine.

So disengag'd from sinne and sicknesse,
    Touch it with thy celestiall quicknesse,
        That it may hang and move
          After thy love.

Then with our trinitie of light,
    Motion, and heat, let's take our flight
        Unto the place where thou
          Before didst bow.

Get me a standing there, and place
    Among the beams, which crown the face
        Of him, who dy'd to part
          Sinne and my heart:

That so among the rest I may
    Glitter, and curle, and winde as they:
        That winding is their fashion
           Of adoration.

Sure thou wilt joy, by gaining me
    To flie home like a laden bee
        Unto that hive of beams
           And garland-streams.

Virtue

SWEET DAY, so cool, so calm, so bright,
The bridal of the earth and sky,
The dew shall weep thy fall tonight;
          For thou must die.

Sweet rose, whose hue angry and brave
Bids the rash gazer wipe his eye,
Thy root is ever in its grave,
          And thou must die.

Sweet spring, full of sweet days and roses,
A box where sweets compacted lie,
My music shows ye have your closes,
          And all must die.

Only a sweet and virtuous soul,
Like season'd timber, never gives;
But though the whole world turn to coal,
          Then chiefly lives.

Love

LOVE BADE me welcome; yet my soul drew back,
                Guilty of dust and sin.
But quick-ey'd Love, observing me grow slack
                From my first entrance in,
Drew nearer to me, sweetly questioning
                If I lack'd any thing.

'A guest', I answer'd, 'worthy to be here.'
                Love said, 'You shall be he.'
'I the unkind, ungrateful? Ah my dear,
                I cannot look on thee.'
Love took my hand, and smiling did reply,
                'Who made the eyes but I?'

'Truth lord, but I have marr'd them; let my shame
                Go where it doth deserve.'
'And know you not', says Love, 'who bore the blame?'
                'My dear, then I will serve.'
'You must sit down,' says Love, 'and taste my meat.'
                So I did sit and eat.

The Flower

HOW FRESH, O Lord, how sweet and clean
Are thy returns! even as the flowers in spring,
    To which, besides their own demean,
The late-past frosts tributes of pleasure bring;
          Grief melts away
          Like snows in May,
    As if there were no such cold thing.

    Who could have thought my shrivelled heart
Could have recovered greenness? It was gone
    Quite underground; as flowers depart
To see their mother-root, when they have blown;
          Where they together
          All the hard weather,
    Dead to the world, keep house unknown.

    These are thy wonders, Lord of power,
Killing and quickening, bringing down to hell
    And up to heaven in an hour;
Making a chiming of a passing-bell.
          We say amiss
          This or that is;
    Thy word is all, if we could spell.

    O that I once past changing were,
Fast in thy Paradise, where no flower can wither!
    Many a spring I shoot up fair,
Offering at heaven, growing and groaning thither;
          Nor doth my flower
          Want a spring shower,
    My sins and I joining together.

    But while I grow in a straight line,
Still upwards bent, as if heaven were mine own,
    Thy anger comes, and I decline;
What frost to that? what pole is not the zone
          Where all things burn,
          When thou dost turn,

And the least frown of thine is shown?

And now in age I bud again,
After so many deaths I live and write;
    I once more smell the dew and rain,
And relish versing. O, my only light,
              It cannot be
              That I am he
On whom thy tempests fell all night.

These are thy wonders, Lord of love,
To make us see we are but flowers that glide;
    Which when we once can find and prove,
Thou hast a garden for us, where to bide.
              Who would be more,
              Swelling through store,
Forfeit their Paradise by their pride.

Easter-Wings

LORD, WHO createst man in wealth and
store,
Though foolishly he lost the same,
Decaying more and more,
Til he became
Most poore:
With thee
O let me rise
As larks, harmoniously,
And sing this day thy victories:
Then shall the fall further the flight in
me.

My tender age in sorrow did beginne:
And still with sicknesses and shame
Thou didst so punish sinne,
That I became
Most thinne,
With thee
Let me combine
And feel this day thy victorie:
For, if I imp my wing on thine,
Affliction shall advance the flight in
me.

RICHARD CRASHAW

(1613?-1649)

Hymn of the Nativity (Full Chorus)

WELLCOME ALL WONDERS in one sight!
Aeternity shut in a span.
  Sommer in Winter, Day in Night.
Heaven in earth, and GOD in MAN.
  Great little one! whose all-embracing birth
Lifts earth to heaven, stoopes heav'n to earth.

WELLCOME. Though not to gold nor silk,
To more than Cæsar's birth right is;
  Two sister-seas of Virgin-Milk,
With many a rarely-temper'd kisse
  That breathes at once both MAID and MOTHER,
Warmes in the one, cooles in the other.

WELLCOME, though not to those gay flyes
Gilded with' Beames of earthly kings;
  Slippery soules in smiling eyes;
But to poor Shepherds, home-spun things:
  Whose Wealth's their flock; whose wit, to be
Well read in their simplicity.

Yet when young April's husband showrs
Shall blesse the fruitfull Maia's bed,
  We'll bring the First-born of her flowrs
To kisse thy FEET and crown thy HEAD.
  To thee, dread Lamb! whose love must keep
The shepheards, more than they the sheep.

TO THEE, meek Majesty! soft KING
Of simple GRACES and sweet LOVES.
  Each of us his lamb will bring

✧ *41*

Each his pair of slyver Doves;
    Till burnt at last in fire of Thy fair eyes,
Our selves become our own best Sacrifice.

To the Countess, Persuading Her to Resolution in Religion

WHAT HEAVEN-INTREATED HEART is This
Stands trembling at the gate of blisse:
Holds fast the door, yet dares not venture
Fairly to open it, and enter,
Whose DEFINITION is a Doubt
Twixt Life & Death, twixt In & Out.
Say, lingering fair! why comes the birth
Of your brave soul so slowly forth?
Plead your pretences (o you strong
In weakness!) why you choose so long
In labour of yourself to ly,
No daring quite to live nor dy?
Ah linger not, lov'd soul! No,
Who grant at last, a long time tryd
And did his best to have deny'd.
What magick bolt, what mystick Barres
Maintain the will in these strange warres!
What fatal, yet fantastick, bands
Keep Thee free Heart from it's own hands!
So when the year takes cold, we see
Poor waters their own prisoners be.
Fetter'd, & lockt up fast they ly
In a sad self-captivity.
The' astonisht nymphs their flood's strange fate deplore,
To see themselves their on severer shore.
Thou that alone canst thaw this cold,
And fetch the heart from it's strong Hold;
Almighty LOVE! end this long war,
And of a meteor make a star.
O fix this fair INDEFINITE.

And 'mongst thy shafts of soveraign light
Choose out that sure decisive dart
Which has the Key of this close heart,
Knows all the corners of 't, & can control
The self-shut cabinet of an unsearcht soul.
O let it be at last, love's hour.
Raise this tall Trophee of thy Powre;
Come once the conquering way; not to confute
But kill this rebel-word, IRRESOLUTE
That so, inspite of all this peevish strength
Of weakness, she may write REVOL'D AT LENGTH,
Unfold at length, unfold fair flowre
And use the season of love's showre,
Meet his well-meaning Wounds, wiseheart!
And hast to drink the wholesome dart.
That healing shaft, which heaven till now
Hath in love's quiver hid for you.
O Dart of love! arrow of light!
O happy you, if it hit right,
It must not fall in vain, it must
Not mark the dry regardless dust.
Fair one, it is your fate; and brings
Eternal worlds upon its wings.
Meet it with wide-spread arms; and see
Its seat your soul's just centre be.
Disabled dull feares; give faith the day.
To save your life, kill your delay
It is love's siege; and sure to be
Your triumph, though his victory.
'Tis cowardice that keeps this field
And want of courage not to yield.
Yield then, O yield, that love may win
The Fort at last, and let life in.
Yield quickly. Lest perhaps you prove
Death's prey, before the prize of love.

This Fort of your fair selfe, if it be not won,
He is repulst indeed; But you are undone.

HENRY VAUGHAN
(1621-1695)

The Retreat

HAPPY THOSE early days! when I
Shined in my Angel-infancy.
Before I understood this place
Appointed for my second race,
Or taught my soul to fancy aught
But a white, celestial thought,
When yet I had not walked above
A mile, or two, from my first love,
And looking back (at that short space,)
Could see a glimpse of his bright-face;
When on some *gilded cloud*, or *flower*
My gazing souls would dwell an hour,
And in those weaker glories spy
Some shadows of eternity;
Before I taught my tongue to wound
My conscience with a sinful sound,
Or had the black art to dispense
A several sin to every sense,
But felt through all this fleshly dress
Bright *shoots* of everlastingness.
   O how I long to travel back
And tread against that ancient track!
That I might once more reach that plain,
Where first I left my glorious train,
From whence the enlightened spirits sees
That shady city of palm trees;
But (ah!) my soul with too much stay
Is drunk, and staggers in the way.
Some men a forward motion love,
But I by backward steps would move,
And when this dust falls to the urn
In that state I came return.

The World

1

I SAW Eternity the other night
Like a great *Ring* of pure and endless light,
      All calm, as it was bright,
And round beneath it, Time in hours, days, years
    Driven by the spheres
Like a vast shadow moved, in which the world
      And all her train were hurled;
The doting lover in his quaintest straining
      Did there complain,
Near him, his lute, his fancy, and his flights,
      Wit's sour delights,
With gloves, and knots the silly snares of pleasure
      Yet his dear treasure
All scattered lay, while he his eyes did pour
      Upon a flower.

2

The darksome states-man hung with weights and woe
Like a thick midnight-fog moved there so slow
      He did nor stay, nor go;
Condemning thoughts (like sad eclipses) scowl
      Upon his soul,
And clouds of crying witnesses without
      Pursued him with one shout.
Yet digged the mole, and lest his ways be found
      Worked under ground,
Where he did clutch his prey, but one did see
      That policy,
Churches and altars fed him, perjuries
      Were gnats and flies,
It rained about him blood and tears, but he
      Drank them as free.

3

The fearful miser on a heap of rust
Sat pining all his life there, did scarce trust
    His own hands with the dust,
Yet would not place one piece above, but lives
    In fear of thieves.
Thousands there were as frantic as himself
    And hugged each one his pelf,
The down-right epicure placed heaven in sense
    And scorned pretence
While others slipped into a wide excess
    Said little less;
The weaker sort slight, trivial wares enslave
    Who think them brave,
And poor, despised truth sat counting by
    Their victory.

4

Yet some, who all this while did weep and sing,
And sing, and weep, soared up into the *Ring*,
    But most would use no wing.
O fools (said I,) thus to prefer dark night
    Before true light,
To live in grots, and caves, and hate the day
    Because it shows the way,
The way which from this dead and dark abode
    Leads up to God,
A way where you might tread the sun, and he
    More bright than he.
But as I did their madness so discuss
    One whispered thus,
This ring the bride-groom did for none provide
    But for his bride.

'They are all gone into the world of light!'

THEY ARE all gone into the world of light!
    And I alone sit ling'ring here;
Their very memory is fair and bright,
       And my sad thoughts doth clear.

It glows and glitters in my cloudy breast
    Like stars upon some gloomy grove,
Or those faint beams in which this hill is dressed,
    After the sun's remove.

I see them walking in an air of glory,
    Whose light doth trample on my days:
My days, which are at best but dull and hoary,
       Mere glimmering and decays.

O holy hope! and high humility,
    High as the heavens above!
These are your walks, and you have showed them me
       To kindle my cold love,

Dear, beauteous death! the jewel of the just,
    Shining nowhere, but in the dark;
What mysteries do lie beyond thy dust;
       Could man outlook that mark!

He that hath found some fledged bird's nest, may know
    At first sight, if the bird be flown;
But what fair well, or grove he sings in now,
       That is to him unknown.

And yet, as Angels in some brighter dreams
    Call to the soul, when man doth sleep:
So some strange thoughts transcend our wonted themes,
       And into glory peep.

If a star were confined into a tomb
    Her captive flames must needs burn there;
But when the hand that locked her up, gives room

✧ *49*

She'll shine through all the sphere.

O Father of eternal life, and all
    Created glories under thee!
Resume thy spirit from this world of thrall
      Into true liberty.

Either disperse these mists, which blot and fill
    My perspective (still) as they pass,
Or else remove me hence unto that hill,
      Where I shall need no glass.

The Morning-Watch

O JOYS! infinite sweetness! with what flowers,
And shoots of glory, my soul breaks, and buds!
        All the long hours
        Of night, and rest
        Through the still shrouds
        Of sleep, and clouds,
     This dew fell on my breast;
        Of how it *blows*,
And *spirits* all my earth! hark! In what rings,
And *hymning circulations* the quick world
        Awakes, and sings;
        The rising winds,
        And falling springs,
        Birds, beasts, all things
     A doe him in their kinds.
        Thus all is hurled
In sacred *hymns*, and *order*, the great *chime*
And *symphony* of nature. Prayer is
        The world in tune,
        A spirit-voice,
        And vocal joys
     Whose *echo is* heaven's bliss.
        O let me climb
When I lie down! The pious soul by night
Is like a clouded star, whose beams though said
        To shed their light
        Under some cloud
        Yet are above,
        And shine, and move
     Beyond that misty shroud.
        So in my bed
That curtained grave, though sleep, like ashes, hide
My lamp, and life, both shall in thee abide.

Peace

MY SOUL, there is a country
    Far beyond the stars,
Where stands a winged sentry
    All skillful in the wars,
There above noise, and danger
    Sweet peace sits crowned with smiles,
And one born in a manger
    Commands the beauteous files,
He is thy gracious friend,
    And (O my soul awake!)
Did in pure love descend
    To die here for thy sake,
If thou canst get but thither,
    There grows the flower of peace,
The rose that cannot wither,
    Thy fortress, and thy ease;
Leave then thy foolish ranges;
    For none can thee secure,
But one, who never changes,
    Thy God, thy life, thy cure.

THOMAS TRAHERNE

(1636?-1674)

Wonder

HOW LIKE an angel came I down!
How bright are all things here!
When first among his works I did appear,
Oh, how their Glory me did crown!
The world resembled his Eternity,
In which my soul did walk;
And every thing that I did see
Did with me talk.

The skies in their magnificence,
The lively, lovely air;
Oh, how divine, how soft, how sweet, how fair!
The stars did entertain my sense,
And all the works of God so bright and pure,
So rich and great did seem
As if they ever must endure
In my esteem.

A native health and innocence
Within my bones did grow,
And while my God did all his glories show,
I felt a vigour in my sense
That was all spirit. I within did flow
With seas of life, like wine;
I nothing in the world did know,
But 'twas divine.

Harsh, ragged objects were concealed,
Oppressions, tears, and cries,
Sins, griefs, complaints, dissentions, weeping eyes,
Were hid: and only things revealed
Which heavenly spirits and the angels prize.

The State of Innocence
And Bliss, not trades and poverties,
Did fill my sense.

The streets were paved with golden stones,
The boys and girls were mine;
Oh, how did all their lovely faces shine!
The Sons of Men were Holy Ones,
Joy, Beauty, Welfare did appear to me,
And every thing which here I found,
While like an angel I did see,
Adorned the ground.

Rich diamond, and pearl, and gold
In every place was seen;
Rare splendours, yellow, blue, red, white, and green,
Mine eyes did everywhere behold;
Great Wonders clothed with Glory did appear,
Amazement was my Bliss.
That and my wealth was everywhere:
No Joy to this....

from Centuries of Meditations

NOW TO enjoy the treasures of God in the similitude of God, is the most perfect blessedness God could devise. For the treasures of God are the most perfect treasures, and the manner of God is the most perfect manner. To enjoy therefore the treasures of God after the similitude of God is to enjoy the most perfect treasures in the most perfect manner. Upon which I was infinitely satisfied in God, and knew there was a Deity because I was satisfied. For in exerting himself wholly in achieving thus an infinite Felicity he was infinitely delightful, great and glorious, and my desires so august and insatiable that nothing less than a Deity could satisfy them.

This spectacle once seen, will never be forgotten. It is a great part of the beatific vision. A sight of happiness is happiness. It transforms the Soul and makes it heavenly, it powerfully calls us to communion with God, and weans us from the costumes of this world. It puts a lustre upon God and all his creatures and makes us to see them in a Divine and Eternal Light.

from My Spirit

O JOY! O wonder and delight!
    O sacred mystery!
My Soul a Spirit infinite!
An image of the Deity!
    A pure substantial light!
That Being greatest which doth nothing seem!
Why, 'twas my all, I nothing did esteem
But that alone. A strange mysterious sphere!
    A deep abyss
    That sees and is
The only proper place of Heavenly Bliss.
    To its Creator 'tis so near
      In love and excellence,
        In life and sense,
In greatness, worth, and nature; and so dear,
    In it, without hyperbole,
    The Son and friend of God we see.

    A strange extended orb of Joy,
      Proceeding from within,
    Which did on every side, convey
    Itself, and being nigh of kin
      To Go did every way
Dilate itself even in an instant, and
Like an indivisible centre stand,
At once surrounding all eternity.
    'Twas not a sphere,
    Yet did appear,
One infinite. 'Twas somewhat every where,
    And though it had a power to see
      Far more, yet still it shin'd
      And was a mind
Exerted, for it saw Infinity.
    'Twas not a sphere, but 'twas a might
    Invisible, and yet gave light.

    O wondrous Self! O sphere of light,
      O sphere of joy most fair

O act, O power infinite;
O subtile and unbounded air!
O living or of sight!
Thou which within me art, yet me! Thou eye,
And temple of His whole infinity!
O what a world art Thou! A world within!
All things appear,
All objects are
Alive in Thee! Supersubstantial, rare,
Above themselves, and nigh of kin
To those pure things we find
In His great mind
Who made the world! Tho' now eclipsed by sin
There they are useful and divine,
Exalted there they ought to shine.

WILLIAM BLAKE
(1757-1827)

Song

FRESH FROM the dewy hill, the merry year
Smiles on my head, and mounts his flaming car;
Round my young brows the laurel wreathes a shade,
And rising glories beam around my head.

My feet are wing'd, while o'er the dewy lawn,
I meet my maiden, risen like the morn:
Oh bless those holy feet, like angels' feet;
Oh bless those limbs, beaming with heav'nly light!

Like as an angel glitt'ring in the sky,
In times of innocence, and holy joy;
The joyful shepherd stops his grateful song,
To hear the music of an angel's tongue.

So when she speaks, the voice of Heaven I hear
So when we walk, nothing impure comes near;
Each field seems Eden, and each calm retreat;
Each village seems the haunt of holy feet.

But that sweet village where my black-ey'd maid,
Closes her eyes in sleep beneath night's shade:
Whene'er I enter, more than mortal fire
Burns in my soul, and does my song inspire.

Eternity

HE WHO bends to himself a joy
Does the wingèd life destroy;
But he who kisses the joy as it flies
Lives in eternity's sunrise.

Songs of Innocence

PIPING DOWN the valleys wild,
Piping songs of peasant glee,
On a cloud I saw a child,
And he, laughing, said to me:

'Pipe a song about a lamb!'
So I piped with merry cheer.
'Piper, pipe that song again;'
So I piped: he wept to hear.

'Drop thy pipe, thy happy pipe;
Sing thy songs of happy cheer!'
So I sang the same again,
While he wept with joy to hear.

'Piper, sit thee down and write
In a book, that all may read.'
So he vanished from my sight;
And I plucked a hollow reed,

And I made a rural pen,
And I stain'd the water clear,
And I wrote my happy songs
Every child may joy to hear.

To the Evening Star

THOU FAIR-HAIR'D angel of the evening,
Now, whilst the sun rests on the mountains, light
Thy bright torch of love; thy radiant crown
Put on, and smile upon our evening bed!
Smile on our loves, and while thou drawest the
Blue curtains of the sky, scatter thy silver dew
On every flower that shuts its sweet eyes
In timely sleep. Let thy west wind sleep on
The lake; speak silence with thy glimmering eyes,
And wash the dusk with silver. Soon, full soon,
Dost thou withdraw; then the wolf rages wide,
And then the lion glares through the dun forest:
The fleeces of our flocks are cover'd with
Thy sacred dew: protect them with thine influence!

WILLIAM WORDSWORTH
(1770-1850)

from Intimations of Immortality
from Recollection of Early Childhood

      O JOY! that in our embers
      Is something that doth live,
      That nature yet remembers
      What was so fugitive!
The thought of our past years in me doth breed
Perpetual benediction: not indeed
For that which is most worthy to be blest;
Delight and liberty, the simple creed
Of Childhood, whether busy or at rest,
With new-fledged hope still fluttering in his breast: –
      Not for these I raise
      The song of thanks and praise;
    But for those obstinate questiongs
    Of sense and outward things,
    Fallings from us, vanishings;
    Blank misgivings of a Creature
Moving about in worlds not realized,
High instincts before which our mortal Nature
Did tremble like a guilty Thing surprised:
      But for those first affections,
      Those shadowy recollections,
    Which, be they what they may,
Are yet the fountain light of all our day,
Are yet a master light of all our seeing;
    Upholds us, cherish, and have power to make
Our noisy years seem moments in the being
Of the eternal Silence: truths that wake,
      To perish never;
Which neither listlessness, nor mad endeavour,
      Nor Man nor Boy,
Not all that is at enmity with joy,

Can utterly abolish or destroy!
   Hence in a season of calm weather
   Though inland far we be,
Our Souls have sight of that immortal sea
   Which brought us thither,
And see the Children sport upon the shore,
And hear the mighty waters rolling evermore.

Then sing, ye Birds, sing, sing a joyous song!
   And let the young Lambs bound
   As to the tabor's sound!
We in thought will join your throng,
   Ye that pipe and ye that play,
   Ye that through your hearts today
   Feel the gladness of the May!
What though the radiance which was once so bright
Be now for ever taken from my sight,
   Though nothing can bring back the hour
Of splendour in the grass, of glory in the flower;
   We will grieve not, rather find
   Strength in what remains behind;
   In the primal sympathy
   Which having been must ever be;
   In the soothing thoughts that spring
   Out of human suffering;
   In the faith that looks through death,
In years that bring the philosophic mind.

And O, ye Fountains, Meadows, Hills, and Groves,
Forbode not any severing of our loves!
Yet in my heart of hearts I feel your might;
I only have relinquished one delight
To live beneath your more habitual sway.
I love the Brooks which down their channels fret,
Even more than when I tripped lightly as they;
The innocent brightness of a new-born Day
   Is lovely yet;
The Clouds that gather round the setting sun
Do take a sober colouring from an eye
That hath kept watch o'er man's mortality;
Another race hath been. And other palms are won.

Thanks to the human heart by which we live,
Thanks to its tenderness, its joys, and fears,
To me the meanest flower that blows can give
Thoughts that do often lie too deep for tears.

from *Lines Composed a Few Miles Above Tintern Abbey*

            ...FOR I have learned
To look on nature, not as in the hour
Of thoughtless youth; but hearing oftentimes
The still, sad music of humanity,
Nor harsh nor grating, though of ample power
To chasten and subdue. And I have felt
A presence that disturbs me with the joy
Of elevated thoughts; a sense sublime
Of something far more deeply interfused,
Whose dwelling is the light of setting suns,
And the round ocean and the living air,
And the blue sky, and in the mind of man:
A motion and a spirit, that impels
All thinking things, all objects of all thought,
And rolls through all things. Therefore am I still
A lover of the meadows and the woods,
And mountains; and of all that we behold
From this green earth; of all the mighty world
Of eye, and ear, - both what they half create,
And what perceive; well pleased to recognize
In nature and the language of the sense,
The anchor of my purest thoughts, the nurse,
The guide, the guardian of my heart, and soul
Of all my moral being.

SAMUEL TAYLOR COLERIDGE
(1772-1834)

from This Lime-Tree Bower My Prison

A DELIGHT!
Comes sudden on my heart, and I am glad
As I myself were there! Nor in this bower,
This little lime-tree bower, have I not mark'd
Much that has sooth'd me. Pale beneath the blaze
Hung the transparent foliage; and I watch'd
Some broad and sunny leaf, and lov'd to see
The shadow of the leaf and stem above
Dappling its sunshine! And that walnut-tree
Was richly ting'd, and a deep radiance lay
Full on the ancient ivy, which usurps
Those fronting elms, and now, with blackest mass
Makes their dark branches gleam a lighter hue
Through the late twilight: and though now the bat
Wheels silent by, and not a swallow twitters,
Yet still the solitary humble-bee
Sings in the bean-flower! henceforth I shall know
That Nature ne'er deserts the wise and pure;
No plot so narrow, be but Nature there,
No waste so vacant, but may well employ
Each faculty of sense, and keep the heart
Awake to Love and Beauty! and sometimes
'Tis well to be bereft of promis'd good,
That we may lift the soul and contemplate
With lively joy the joys we cannot share.
My gentle-hearted Charles! when the last rook
Beat its straight path along the dusky air
Homewards, I blest it! deeming its black wing
(Now a dim speck, now vanishing in light)
Had cross'd the mighty Orb's dilated glory,
While thou stood'st gazing; or, when all was still,
Flew creeking o'er thy head, and had a charm

For thee, my gentle-hearted Charles, to whom
No sound is dissonant which tells of life.

PERCY BYSSHE SHELLEY
(1792-1822)

from Epipsychidion

SERAPH OF Heaven! too gentle to be human,
Veiling beneath that radiant form of Woman
All that is insupportable in thee
Of light, and love, and immortality!
Sweet benediction in the eternal Curse!
Veiled Glory of this lampless Universe!
Thou Moon beyond the clouds! Thou living Form
Among the Dead! Thou Star above the Storm!
Thou Wonder, and thou beauty, and thou Terror!
Thou Harmony of Nature's art! Thou Mirror
In whom, as in the splendour of the sun,
All shapes look glorious which thou gazest on!
Ay, even the dim words which obscure thee now
Flash, lightning-like, with unaccustomed glow;
I pray thee that thou blot from this sad song
All of its much mortality and wrong,
With those clear drops, which start like sacred dew
From the twin lights thy sweet soul darkens through,
Weeping, till sorrow becomes ecstasy:
Then smile on it, so that it may not die.

To a Skylark

HAIL TO thee, blithe Spirit!
  Bird thou never wert,
That from heaven, or near it,
  Pourest thy full heart
In profuse strains of unpremeditated art.

Higher still and higher
  From the earth thou springest
Like a cloud of fire;
  The blue deep thou wingest,
And singing still dost soar, and soaring ever singest.

In the golden lightning
  Of the sunken sun,
O'er which clouds are bright'ning,
  Thou dost float and run;
Like an unbodied joy whose race is just begun.

The pale purple even
  Melts around thy flight;
Like a star of heaven,
  In the broad daylight
Thou art unseen, but yet I hear thy shrill delight,

Keen as are the arrows
  Of that silver sphere,
Whose intense lamp narrows
  In the white dawn clear
Until we hardly see - we feel that it is there.

All the earth and air
With thy voice is loud,
As, when night is bare,
  From one lonely cloud
The moon rains out her beams, and Heaven is overflowed.

What thou art we know not;
    What is most like thee?
From rainbow clouds there flow not
    Drops so bright to see
As from thy presence showers a rain of melody.

Like a Poet hidden
    In the light of thought,
Singing hymns unbidden,
    Till the world is wrought
To sympathy with hopes and fears it heeded not:

Like a high-born maiden
    In a palace-tower,
Soothing her love-laden
    Soul in secret hour
With music sweet as love, which overflows her bower

Like a glow-worm golden
    In a dell of dew,
Scattering unbeholden
    Its aëreal hue
Among the flowers and grass, which screen it from the view!

Like a rose embowered
    In its own green leaves,
By warm winds deflowered,
    Till the scent it gives
Makes faint with too much sweet those heavy-wingèd thieves:

Sound of vernal showers
    On the twinkling grass,
Rain-awakened flowers,
    All that ever was
Joyous, and clear, and fresh, thy music doth surpass:

Teach us, Sprite or Bird,
    What sweet thoughts are thine:
I have never heard
    Praise of love or wine
That panted forth a flood of rapture so divine.

✦ 70

Chorus Hymeneal,
   Or triumphal chant,
Matched with thine would be all
   But an empty vaunt,
A thing wherein we feel there is some hidden want.

What objects are the fountains
   Of thy happy strain?
What fields, or waves, or mountains?
   What shapes or sky or plain?
What love of thine own kind? what ignorance of pain?

With thy clear keen joyance
   Languor cannot be:
Shadow of annoyance
   Never came near thee:
Thou lovest – but ne'er knew love's sad satiety.

Waking or asleep,
   Thou of death must deem
Things more true and deep
   Than we mortals dream,
Or how could thy notes flow in such a crystal stream?

We look before and after,
   And pine for what is not:
Our sincerest laughter
   With some pain is fraught;
Our sweetest songs are those that tell of saddest thought.

Yet if we could scorn
   Hate, and pride, and fear;
If we were things born
   Not to shed a tear,
I know not how thy joy we ever should come near.

Better than all measures
   Of delightful sound,
Better than all treasures
   That in books are found,

Thy skill to poet were, thou scorner of the ground!

Teach me half the gladness
   That thy brain must know,
Such harmonious madness
   From my lips would flow
The world should listen then – as I am listening now.

Hymn of Apollo

I

THE SLEEPLESS Hours who watch me as I lie,
   Curtained with star-inwoven tapestries
From the broad moonlight of the sky,
   Fanning the busy dreams from my dim eyes, –
Waken me when their Mother, the gray Dawn,
Tells them that dreams and that the moon is gone.

II

Then I arise, and climbing heaven's blue dome,
   I walk over the mountains and the waves,
Leaving my robe upon the ocean foam;
   My footsteps pave the clouds with fire; the caves
Are filled with my bright presence, and the air
Leaves the green Earth to my embraces bare.

III

The sunbeams are my shafts, with which I kill
   Deceit, that loves the night and fears the day;
All men who do or even imagine ill
   Fly me, and from the glory of my ray
Good minds and open actions take new might,
Until diminished by the reign of Night.

IV

I feed the clouds, the rainbows and the flowers
   With their æthereal colours; the moon's globe
And the pure stars in their eternal bowers
   Are cinctured with my power as with a robe;
Whatever lamps on Earth or heaven may shine
Are portions of one power, which is mine.

V

I stand at noon upon the peak of Heaven,
    Then with unwilling steps I wander down
Into the clouds of the Atlantic even;
    For grief that I depart they weep and frown:
What look is more delightful than the smile
With which I soothe them from the western isle?

VI

I am the eye with which the Universe
    Beholds itself and knows itself divine;
All harmony of instrument or verse,
    All prophecy, all medicine is mine,
All light of art or nature; – to my song
Victory and praise in its own right belong.

JOHN KEATS
(1795-1821)

Ode to Psyche

O GODDESS! hear these tuneless numbers, wrung
    By sweet enforcement and remembrance dear,
And pardon that thy secrets should be sung
    Even into thine own soft-conched ear:
Surely I dreamt to-day, or did I see
    The winged Psyche with awaken'd eyes?
I wander'd in a forest thoughtlessly,
    And, on the sudden, fainting with surprise,
Saw two fair creatures, couched side by side
    In deepest grass, beneath the whisp'ring roof
    Of leaves and trembled blossoms, where there ran
        A brooklet, scarce espied:

'Mid hush'd, cool-rooted flowers, fragrant-eyed,
    Blue, silver-white, and budded Tyrian,
They lay calm-breathing on the bedded grass;
    Their arms embraced, and their pinions too:
    Their lips touch'd not, but had not bade adieu,
As if disjoined by soft-handed slumber,
And ready still past kisses to outnumber
    At tender eye-dawn of aurorean love:
        The winged boy I knew;
    But who wast thou, O happy, happy dove?
        His Psyche true!

O latest born and loveliest vision far
    Of all Olympus' faded hierarchy!
Fairer than Phoebe's sapphire-region'd star,
Or Vesper, amorous glow-worm of the sky;
Fairer than these, though temple thou hast none,
        Nor altar heap'd with flowers;
Nor virgin-choir to make delicious moan

Upon the midnight hours;
No voice, no lute, no pipe, no incense sweet
    From chain-swung censer teeming;
No shrine, no grove, no oracle, no heat
    Of pale-mouth'd prophet dreaming.

O brightest! though too late for antique vows,
    Too, too late for the fond believing lyre,
When holy were the haunted forest boughs,
    Holy the air, the water, and the fire;
Yet even in these days so far retir'd
    From happy pieties, thy lucent fans,
    Fluttering among the faint Olympians,
I see, and sing, by my own eyes inspir'd.
So let me be thy choir, and make a moan
                Upon the midnight hours;
Thy voice, thy lute, thy pipe, thy intense sweet
    From swinged censer teeming;
Thy shrine, thy grove, thy oracle, thy heat
    Of pale-mouth'd prophet dreaming.

Yes, I will by thy priest, and build a fane
    In some untrodden region of my mind,
Where branched thoughts, new grown with pleasant pain,
Instead of pines shall murmur in the wind:
Far, far around shall those dark-cluster'd trees
    Fledge the wild--ridged mountains steep by steep;
And there by zephyrs, streams, and birds, and bees,
    The moss-lain dryads shall be lull'd to sleep;
And in the midst of this wide quietness
    A rosy sanctuary will I dress
With the wreath'd trellis of a working brain,
    With buds, and bells, and stars without a name.
With all the gardener Fancy e'er could feign,
    Who breeding flowers, will never breed the same:
And there shall be for thee all soft delight
    That shadowy thought can win,
A bright torch, and a casement ope at night,
    To let the warm Love in!

from Endymion

Book I

A THING of beauty is a joy for ever:
Its loveliness increases; it will never
Pass into nothingness; but still will keep
A bower quiet for us, and a sleep
Full of sweet dreams, and health and quiet breathing.
Therefore, on every morrow, are we wreathing
A flowery band to bind us to the earth,
Spite of despondence, of the inhuman dearth
Of noble natures, of the gloomy days,
Of all the unhealthy and o'er-darkened ways
Made for our searching: yes, inspite of all,
Some shape of beauty moves away the pall
From our dark spirits. Such the sun, the moon,
Trees old and young, sprouting a shady boon
For simple sheep; and such are daffodils
With the green world they live in; and clear rills
That for themselves a cooling covert make
'Gainst the hot season; the mid-forest brake,
Rich with a sprinkling of fair musk-rose blooms:
And such too is the grandeur of the dooms
We have imagined for the mighty dead;
All lovely tales that we have heard or read:
An endless fountain of immortal drink,
Pouring unto us from the heaven's brink.

Nor do we merely feel these essences
For one short hour; no, even as the trees
That whisper round a temple become soon
Dear as the temple's self, so does the moon,
The passion poesy, glories infinite,
Haunt us till they become a cheering light
Unto our souls, and bound to us so fast,
That, whether there be shine, or gloom o'ercast,
They always must be with us, or we die.

[...]

O magic sleep! O comfortable bird,
That broodest o'er the troubled sea of the mind
Till it is hush'd and smooth! O unconfin'd
Restraint! imprisoned liberty! great key
To golden palaces, strange minstrelsy,
Fountains grotesque, new trees, bespangled caves,
Echoing grottoes, full of tumbling waves
And moonlight; aye, to all the mazy world
Of silvery enchantment! – who, upfurl'd
Beneath thy drowsy wing a triple hour,
But renovates and lives? – Thus, in the bower,
Endymion was calm'd to life again.

RALPH WALDO EMERSON
(1803-1882)

Merlin (I)

THY TRIVIAL harp will ever please
Or fill my craving ear;
Its chords should ring as blows the breeze,
Free, peremptory, clear,
No jingling serenader's art,
Nor tinkle of piano strings,
Can make the wild blood start
In its mystic springs.
The kingly bard
Must smite the chords rudely and hard,
As with hammer or with mace;
That they may render back
Artful thunder, which conveys
Secrets of the solar track,
Sparks of the supersolar blaze.
Merlin's blows are strokes of fate,
Chiming with the forest tone,
When boughs buffet boughs in the wood;
Chiming with the gasp and moan
Of the ice-imprisoned flood;
With the pulse of manly hearts;
With the the voice of orators;
With the din of city arts;
With the cannonade of wars;
With the marches of the brave;
And prayers of might from martyr's cave.

Great is the art,
Great be the manners, of the bard.
He shall not his brain encumber
With the coil of rhythm and number;
But, leaving rule and pale forethought,

He shall aye climb
For his rhyme.
"Pass in, pas in," the angels say,
"In to the upper doors,
Nor count compartments of the flows,
But mount to paradise
By the stairway of surprise."

Blameless master of the games,
King of sport that never shames,
He shall daily joy dispense
His in song's sweet influence.
Forms more cheerly live and go,
What time the subtle mind
Sings aloud the tune whereto
Their pules beat,
And march their feet,
And their members are combined.

By Sybarites beguiled,
He shall no task decline;
Merlin's mighty line
Extremes of nature reconciled, -
Bereaved a tyrant of his will,
And made the lion mild.
Songs can the tempest still.
Scattered on the stormy air,
Mould the year to fair increase,
And bright in poetic peace.

He shall not seek to weave,
In weak, unhappy times,
Efficacious rhymes;
Wait his returning strength.
Bird that from the nadir's floor
To the zenith's top can soar, -
The soaring orbit of the muse exceeds that journey's length.

Nor profane affect to hit
Or compass that, by meddling wit,
Which only the propitious mind

Publishes when 't is inclined.
There are open hours
When the God's will sallies free,
And the dull idiot might see
The flowing fortunes of a thousand years; –
Sudden, at unawares,
Self-moved, fly-to-the doors,
Nor sword of angels could reveal
What they conceal.

ELIZABETH BARRETT BROWNING
(1806-1861)

"We sow the glebe, we reap the corn"

WE SOW the glebe, we reap the corn,
   We build the house where we may rest,
And then, at moments, suddenly
We look up to the great wide sky,
Inquiring wherefore we were born,
   For earnest or for jest?

The senses folding thick and dark
   About the stifled soul within,
We guess diviner things beyond,
And yearn to them with yearning fond;
We strike out blindly to a mark
   Believed in, but not seen.

We vibrate to the pant and thrill
   Wherewith Eternity has curled
In serpent-twine about God's seat:
While, freshening upward to His feet,
In gradual growth His full-leaved will
 Expands from world to world.

And, in the tumult and excess
   Of act and passion under sun,
We sometimes hear – oh, soft and far,
As silver star did touch with star,
The kiss of Peace and Righteousness
   Through all things that are done.

God keeps His holy mysteries
   Just on the outside of man's dream;
In dispason slow, we think
To hear their pinions rise and sink,

While they float pure beneath His eyes,
    Like swans adown a stream.

Abstractions, are they from the forms
    Of His great beauty? – exaltations
From His great glory? – strong previsions
Of what we shall be? – intuitions
Of what we are – in calms and storms
    Beyond our peace and passions?

Things nameless! which, in passing so,
    Do stroke us with a subtle grace;
We say, 'Who passes?' – they are dumb;
We cannot see them go or come,
Their touches fall soft, cold, as snow
    Upon a blind man's face.

Yes, touching so they draw above
    Our common thoughts to Heaven's unknown;
Our daily joy and pain advance
To a divine significance,
Our human love – O mistral love,
    That light is not its own!

And sometimes horror chills our blood
    To be so near such mystic Things,
And we wrap round us for defence
Our purple manners, moods of sense –
As angels from the face of God
    Stand hidden in their wings.

And sometimes through life's heavy wound
    We grope for them, with strangled breath
We stretch our hands abroad and try
To reach them in our agony;
And widen, so, the broad life-wound
    Soon large enough for death.

HENRY WADSWORTH LONGFELLOW
(1807-1882)

Hymn to the Night

I HEARD the trailing garments of the Night
    Sweep through her marble halls!
I saw her sable skirts all fringed with light
    From the celestial walls!

I felt her presence, by its spell of might.
    Stoop o'er me from above;
The calm, majestic presence of the Night,
    As of the one I love.

I heard the sounds of sorrow and delight,
    The manifold, soft chimes,
That fill the haunted chambers of the Night,
    Like some old poet's rhymes.

From the cool cisterns of the midnight air
    My spirit drank repose;
The fountain of perpetual peace flows there, –
    From those deep cisterns flows.

O holy Night! from thee I learn to bear
What man has borne before!
Thou layest thy finger on the lips of Care,
    And they complain no more.

Peace! Peace! Orestes-like I breathe this prayer!
    Descend with broad-winged flight,
The welcome, the thrice-prayed for, the most fair,
    The best-loved Night!

EMILY BRONTE
(1818-1848)

"No coward soul is mine"

NO COWARD soul is mine,
No trembler in the world's storm-troubled sphere:
I see Heaven's glories shine,
And faith shines equal, arming me from fear.

O God within my breast,
Almighty, ever-present Deity!
Life – that in me has rest,
As I – undying Life – have power in Thee!

Vain are the thousand creeds
That move men's hearts: unutterably vain;
Worthless as withered weeds,
Or idlest froth amid the boundless main,

To waken doubt in one
Holding so fast by Thine infinity;
So surely anchored on
The steadfast rock of immortality.

With wide-embracing love
Thy spirit animates eternal years,
Pervades and broods above,
Changes, sustains, dissolves, creates, and tears.

Though earth and man were gone,
And suns and universes ceased to be,
And Thou were left alone,
Every existence would exist in Thee.

There is not room for Death,

Nor atom that his might could render void:
Thou – THOU art Being and Breath,
And what THOU art may never be destroyed.

To the Bluebell

SACRED WATCHER, wave thy bells!
Fair hill flower and woodland child!
Dear to me in deep green dells –
Dearest on the mountains wild.

Bluebell, even as all divine
I have seen my darling shine –
Bluebell, even as wan and frail
I have seen my darling fail –
Thou hast found a voice for me,
And soothing words are breathed by thee.

Thus they murmur, "Summer's sun
Warms me till my life is done.
Would I rather choose to die
Under winter's ruthless sky?

"Glad I bloom and calm I fade;
Weeping twilight dews my bed;
Mourner, mourner, dry thy tears –
Sorrow comes with lengthened years!"

WALT WHITMAN
(1819-892)

On the Beach at Night Alone

ON THE beach at night alone,
As the old mother sways her to and fro singing her husky song,
As I watch the bright stars shining, I think a thought of the clef of
the universes and of the future.
A vast similitude interlocks all,
All spheres, grown, ungrown, small, large, suns, moons, planets,
All distances of place however wide,
All distances of time, all inanimate forms,
All souls, all living bodies though they be ever so different, or in
different worlds,
All gaseous, watery, vegetable, mineral processes, the fishes, the
brutes,
All nations, colors, barbarisms, civilizations, languages,
All identities, that have existed or may exist on this globe, or any
globe,
All lives and deaths, all of the past, present, future,
This vast similitude spans them, and always has spann'd,
And shall forever span them and compactly hold and enclose
them.

I Sing the Body Electric

I SING the body electric;
The armies of those I love engirth me, and I engirth them;
They will not let me off till I go with them, respond to them,
And discorrupt them, and charge them full with the
                                          charge of the soul.

Was it doubted that those who corrupt their own bodies
                                          conceal themselves;
And if those who defile the living are as bad as they
                                          who defile the dead?
And if the body does not do as much as the soul?
And if the body were not the soul, what is the soul?

2

The love of the body of man or woman balks account –
                                          the body itself balks account;
That of the male is perfect, and that of the female is
                                          perfect.

The expression of the face balks account,
But the expression of a well-made man appears not only
                                          in his face;
It is in his limbs and joints also, it is curiously in
                                          the joints of his hips and wrists;
It is in his walk, the carriage of his neck, the flex
                                 of his waist and knees – dress does not hide him;
The strong, sweet, supple quality he has, strikes
                                 through the cotton and flannel;
To see him pass conveys as much as the best poem,
                                          perhaps more;
You linger to see his back, and the back of his neck
                                          and shoulder-side.

The sprawl and fulness of babes, the bosoms and heads
     of women, the folds of their dress, their style as we pass in
     the street, the contour of their shape downwards,
The swimmer naked in the swimming-bath, seen as he

swims through the transparent green-shine, or lies with his
face up, and rolls silently to and fro in the heave of the water,
The bending forward and backward of rowers in row-boats
                              – the horseman in his saddle,
Girls, mothers, house-keepers, in all their
                              performances,
The group of laborers seated at noon-time with their
                    open dinner-kettles, and their wives waiting,
The female soothing a child – the farmer's daughter in
                              the garden or cow-yard,
The young fellow hoeing corn – the sleigh-driver
                    guiding his six horses through the crowd,
The wrestle of wrestlers, two apprentice-boys, quite grown,
     lusty, good-natured, native-born, out on the vacant lot at
                              sundown, after work,
The coats and caps thrown down, the embrace of love
                              and resistance,
The upper-hold and the under-hold, the hair rumpled
                    over and blinding the eyes;
The march of firemen in their own costumes, the play
          of masculine muscle through clean-setting trowsers
                              and waist-straps,
The slow return from the fire, the pause when the bell
          strikes suddenly again, and the listening on the alert,
The natural, perfect, varied attitudes – the bent head,
                    the curv'd neck, and the counting;
Such-like I love – I loosen myself, pass freely, am at
                    the mother's breast with the little child,
Swim with the swimmers, wrestle with wrestlers, march
          in line with the firemen, and pause, listen, and count.

3

I know a man, a common farmer – the father of five sons;
And in them were the fathers of sons – and in them were
                              the fathers of sons.

This man was of wonderful vigor, calmness, beauty of
                              person;
The shape of his head, the pale yellow and white of
          his hair and beard, and the immeasurable meaning of his

black eyes - the richness and breadth of his manners,
These I used to go and visit him to see - he was wise also;
He was six feet tall, he was over eighty years old - his sons
        were massive, clean, bearded, tan-faced, handsome;
They and his daughters loved him - all who saw him loved him;
They did not love him by allowance - they loved him with
        personal love;
He drank water only - the blood show'd like scarlet through the
        clear-brown skin of his face;
He was a frequent gunner and fisher - he sail'd his boat himself -
    he had a fine one presented to him by a ship-joiner - he had
    fowling-pieces, presented to him by men that loved him;
When he went with his five sons and many grand-sons to hunt
    or fish, you would pick him out as the most beautiful and
        vigorous of the gang.
You would wish long and long to be with him - you would
    wish to sit by him in the boat, that you and he might
        touch each other.

4

I have perceiv'd that to be with those I like is enough,
To stop in company with the rest at evening is enough,
To be surrounded by beautiful, curious, breathing,
        laughing flesh is enough,
To pass among them, or touch any one, or rest my arm
    ever so lightly round his or her neck for a moment -
        what is this, then?
I do not ask any more delight - I swim in it, as in a sea.

There is something in staying close to men and women, and
    looking on them, and in the contact and odor of them,
        that pleases the soul well;
All things please the soul - but these please the soul well.

5

This is the female form;
A divine nimbus exhales from it from head to foot;
It attracts with fierce undeniable attraction!
I am drawn by its breath as if I were no more than a

helpless vapor – all falls aside but myself and it;
Books, art, religion, time, the visible and solid earth, the
        atmosphere and the clouds, and what was expected of
        heaven or fear'd of hell, are now consumed;
Mad filaments, ungovernable shoots play out of it – the
                response likewise ungovernable;
Hair, bosom, hips, bend of legs, negligent falling hands, all
                diffused – mine too diffused;
Ebb stung by the flow, and flow stung by the ebb – love-flesh
                swelling and deliciously aching;
Limitless limpid jets of love hot and enormous, quivering jelly
        of love, white-blow and delirious juice;
Bridegroom night of love, working surely and softly into the
        prostrate dawn;
Undulating into the willing and yielding day,
Lost in the cleave of the clasping and sweet-flesh'd day.

This is the nucleus – after the child is born of woman,
                the man is born of woman;
This is the bath of birth – this is the merge of small and large,
                and the outlet again.

Be not ashamed, women – your privilege encloses the
                rest, and is the exit of the rest;
You are the gates of the body, and you are the gates of the soul.

The female contains all qualities, and tempers them –
        she is in her place, and moves with perfect balance;
She is all things duly veil'd – she is both passive and active;
She is to conceive daughters as well as sons, and sons
                as well as daughters.

As I see my soul reflected in nature;
As I see through a mist, one with inexpressible completeness
                and beauty,
See the bent head, and arms folded over the breast –
                the female I see.

6

The male is not less the soul, nor more – he too is in his place;
He too is all qualities – he is action and power;
The flush of the known universe is in him;
Scorn becomes him well, and appetite and defiance become him
                    well;
The wildest largest passions, bliss that is utmost, sorrow that is
                    utmost, become him well – pride is for him;
The full-spread pride of man is calming and excellent to the soul;
Knowledge becomes him – he likes it always – he brings
                    everything to the test of himself;
Whatever the survey, whatever the sea and the sail, he strikes
                    soundings at last only here;
(Where else does he strike soundings, except here?)
The man's body is sacred, and the woman's body is sacred;
No matter who it is, it is sacred;
Is it a slave? Is it one of the dull-faced immigrants just landed on
                    the wharf?
Each belongs here or anywhere, just as much as the
                    well-off – just as much as you;
Each has his or her place in the procession.

(All is a procession;
The universe is a procession, with measured and beautiful
                    motion.)

Do you know so much yourself, that you call the slave or the
                    dull-face ignorant?
Do you suppose you have a right to a good sight, and
                    he or she has no right to a sight?
Do you think matter has cohered together from its diffuse float –
        and the soil is on the surface, and water runs, and
        vegetation sprouts,
For you only, and not for him and her?

7

A man's body at auction;
I help the auctioneer – the sloven does not half know his
                    business.

✧ 93

Gentlemen, look on this wonder!
Whatever the bids of the bidders, they cannot be high enough for
it;
For it the globe lay preparing quintillions of years, without one
animal or plant;
For it the revolving cycles truly and steadily roll'd.

In this head the all-baffling brain;
In it and below it, the makings of heroes.

Examine these limbs, red, black, or white – they are so cunning
in tendon and nerve;
They shall be stript, that you may see them.
Exquisite senses, life-lit eyes, pluck, volition,
Flakes of breast-muscle, pliant back-bone and neck, flesh not
flabby, good-sized arms and legs,
And wonders within there yet.

Within there runs blood,
The same old blood!
The same red-running blood!
There swells and jets a heart – there all passions, desires,
reachings, aspirations;
Do you think they are not there because they are not express'd
in parlors and lecture-rooms?

This is not only one man – this is the father of those who shall
be fathers in their turns;
In him the start of populous states and rich republics;
Of him countless immortal lives, with countless embodiments
and enjoyments.

How do you know who shall come from the offspring of his
offspring through the centuries?
Who might you find you have come from yourself, if you
could trace back through the centuries?

8

A woman's body at auction!
She too is not only herself – she is the teeming mother of
                mothers;
She is the bearer of them that shall grow and be mates
                to the mothers.

Have you ever loved the body of a woman?
Have you ever loved the body of a man?
Your father – where is your father?
Your mother – is she living? have you been much with her? and
                has she been much with you?
– Do you not see that these are exactly the same to all, in all
                nations and times, all over the earth?

If any thing is sacred, the human body is sacred,
And the glory and sweet of a man, is the token of manhood
                untainted;
And in man or woman, a clean, strong, firm-fibred body, is
                beautiful as the most beautiful face.

Have you seen the fool that corrupted his own live body? or the
                fool that corrupted her own live body?
For they do not conceal themselves, and cannot conceal
                themselves.

9

O my body! I dare not desert the likes of you in other men and
                women, nor the likes of the parts of you;
I believe the likes of you are to stand or fall with the likes of the
                soul, (and that they are the soul;)
I believe the likes of you shall stand or fall with my poems – and
                that they are poems,
Man's, woman's, child's, youth's, wife's, husband's, mother's,
                father's, young man's, young woman's poems;
Head, neck, hair, ears, drop and tympan of the ears,
Eyes, eye-fringes, iris of the eye, eye-brows, and the waking or
                sleeping of the lids,
Mouth, tongue, lips, teeth, roof of the mouth, jaws, and the

jaw-hinges,
Nose, nostrils of the nose, and the partition,
Cheeks, temples, forehead, chin, throat, back of the neck,
                    neck-slue,
Strong shoulders, manly beard, scapula, hind-shoulders, and the
                    ample side-round of the chest.

Upper-arm, arm-pit, elbow-socket, lower-arm, arm-sinews,
                    arm-bones,
Wrist and wrist-joints, hand, palm, knuckles, thumb, fore-finger,
                    finger-balls, finger-joints, finger-nails,
Broad breast-front, curling hair of the breast, breast-bone,
                    breast-side,
Ribs, belly, back-bone, joints of the back-bone,
Hips, hip-sockets, hip-strength, inward and outward round,
                    man-balls, man-root,
Strong set of thighs, well carrying the trunk above,
Leg-fibres, knee, knee-pan, upper-leg, under leg,
Ankles, instep, foot-ball, toes, toe-joints, the heel;

All attitudes, all the shapeliness, all the belongings of my or
                    your body, or of any one's body, male or female,
The lung-sponges, the stomach-sac, the bowels sweet and clean,
The brain in its folds inside the skull-frame,
Sympathies, heart-valves, palate-valves, sexuality, maternity,
Womanhood, and all that is a woman – and the man that
                    comes from woman,
The womb, the teats, nipples, breast-milk, tears, laughter,
                    weeping, love-looks, love-perturbations and risings,
The voice, articulation, language, whispering, shouting aloud,
Food, drink, pulse, digestion, sweat, sleep, walking, swimming,
Poise on the hips, leaping, reclining, embracing, arm-curving and
                    tightening,
The continual changes of the flex of the mouth, and around
                    the eyes,
The skin, the sun-burnt shade, freckles, hair,
The curious sympathy one feels, when feeling with the hand the
                    naked meat of the body,
The circling rivers, the breath, and breathing it in and out,
The beauty of the waist, and thence of the hips, and thence
                    downward toward the knees,

The thin red jellies within you, or within me – the bones, and the
marrow in the bones,
The exquisite realization of health;
O I say, these are not the parts and poems of the body only, but
of the soul,
O I say now these are the soul!

EMILY DICKINSON
(1830-1886)

"from A Song to David"

GLORIOUS THE sun in mid career;
Glorious th' assembled fires apear;
    Glorious the comet's train:
Glorious the trumpet and alarm;
Glorious th' almighty stretch'd-out arm;
    Glorious th' enraptur'd main;

Glorious the northern lights astream;
Glorious the song, when God's the theme
    Glorious the thunder's roar:
Glorious hosanna from the den;
Glorious the catholic amen;
    Glorious the martyr's gore:

Glorious – more glorious is the crown
Of Him that brought salvation down
    By meekness, call'd thy Son;
Thou that stupendous truth believ'd,
And now the matchless deed's achiev'd,
    Determined, Dared, and Done.

I've Known a Heaven

I'VE KNOWN a heaven, like a Tent –
To wrap its shining Yards –
Pluck up its stakes, and disappear –
Without the sound of Boards
Or Rip of Nail – Or Carpenter –
But just the miles of Stare –
That signalize a Show's Retreat –
In North America –

No Trace – no Figment of the Thing
That dazzled, Yesterday,
No Ring – no Marvel –
Men, and Feats –
Dissolved as utterly –
As Bird's far Navigation
Discloses just a Hue –
A plash of Oars, a Gaiety –
Then swallowed up, of View.

"Behind Me – dips Eternity"

BEHIND ME– dips Eternity –
Before Me - Immortality –
Myself – the Term between –
Death but the Drift of Eastern Gray,
Dissolving into Dawn away,
Before the West begin –

'Tis kingdoms – afterward – they say –
In perfect – pauseless Monarchy –
Whose Prince – is Son of None –
Himself – His Dateless Dynasty –
Himself – Himself diversify –
In Duplicate divine –

'Tis Miracle before Me – then –
'Tis Miracle behind – between –
A Crescent in the Sea –
With Midnight to the North of Her –
And Midnight to the South of Her –
And Maelstrom – in the Sky –

THOMAS HARDY
(1840-1928)

The Darkling Thrush

I LEANT upon a coppice gate
    When Frost was spectre-gray,
And Winter's dregs made desolate
    The weakening eye of day.
The tangled bine-stems scored the sky
    Like strings of broken lyres,
And all mankind that haunted nigh
    Had sought their household fires.

The land's sharp features seemed to be
    The Century's corpse outleant,
His crypt the cloudy canopy,
    The wind his death-lament.
The ancient pulse of germ and birth
    Was shrunken hard and dry,
And every spirit upon earth
    Seemed fervourless as I.

At once a voice arose among
    The bleak twigs overhead
In a full-hearted evensong
    Of joy illimited;
An aged thrush, frail, gaunt, and small,
    In blast-beruffled plume,
Had chosen thus to fling his soul
    Upon the growing gloom.

So little cause for carolings
    Of such ecstatic sound
Was written on terrestrial things
    Afar or nigh around,
That I could think there trembled through

His happy good-night air
Some blessed Hope, whereof he knew
And I was unaware.

Wessex Heights

THERE ARE some heights in Wessex, shaped as if by a kindly hand
For thinking, dreaming, dying on, and at crises when I stand,
Say, on Ingpen Beacon eastward, or on Wylls-Neck westwardly,
I seem where I was before my birth, and after death may be.

In the lowlands I have no comrade, not even the lone man's
                                                friend –
Her who suffereth long and is kind; accepts what he is too weak
                                                to mend:
Down there they are dubious and askance; there nobody thinks
                                                as I,
But mind-chains do not clank where one's next neighbour is the
                                                sky.

In the towns I am tracked by phantoms having weird detective
                                                ways –
Shadows of beings who fellowed with myself of earlier days:
They hang about at places, and they say harsh heavy things–
Men with a wintry sneer, and women with tart disparagings.

Down there I seem to be false to myself, my simple self that was,
And is not now, and I see him watching, wondering what
                                                crass cause
Can have merged him into such a strange continuator as this,
Who yet has something in common with himself, my chrysalis.

I cannot go to the great grey Plain; there's a figure against the
                                                moon,
Nobody sees it but I, and it makes my breast beat out of tune;
I cannot go to the tall-spired town, being barred by the forms
                                                now passed
For everybody but me, in whose long vision they stand there fast.

There's a ghost at Yell'ham Bottom chiding loud at the fall of the
                                                night,
There's a ghost in Froom-vale Vale, thin lipped and vague, in
                                                shroud of white,
There is one in the railway-train whenever I do not want it near,

I see its profile against the pane, saying what I would not hear.

As for one rare fair woman, I am now but a thought of hers,
I enter her mind and another thought succeeds me that she
                                                    prefers;
Yet my love for her in its fulness she herself even did not
                                                    know;
Well, time cures hearts of tenderness, and now I can let her go.

So I am found on Ingpen Beacon, or on Wylls-Neck to the west,
Or else on homely Bulbarrow, or little Pilsdon Crest,
Where men have never cared to haunt, nor women have
                                            walked with me,
And ghosts then keep their distance; and I know some liberty.

GERALD MANLEY HOPKINS
(1844-1889)

The Windhover

I CAUGHT this morning morning's minion, king –
　　dom of daylight's dauphin, dapple-dawn-drawn Falcon, in his
　　　　　　　　　　　　　　　　　riding
　　Of the rolling level underneath him steady air, and striding
High there, how he run upon the rein of a wimpling wing
In his ecstasy! then off, off forth on swing,
　　As a skate's heel sweeps smooth on a bow-end! the hurl and
　　　　　　　　　　　　　　　　gliding
　　Rebuffed the big wind. My heart in hiding
Stirred for a bird, – the achieve of, the mastery of the thing!

Brute beauty and valour and act, oh, air, pride, plume, here
　　Buckle! AND the fire that breaks from thee then, a billion
Times told lovelier, more dangerous, O my chevalier!

No wonder of it: shéer plód makes plough down sillion
Shine, and blue-bleak embers, ah my dear,
　　Fall, gall themselves, and gash gold-vermilion.

Hurrahing in Harvest

SUMMER ENDS now; now, barbarous in beauty, the stooks rise
Around; up above, what wind-walks! what lovely behaviour
Of silk-sack clouds! has wilder, wilful-wavier
Meal-drift moulded ever and melted across skies?

I walk, I lift up, I lift up heart, eyes,
Down all that glory in the heavens to glean our Saviour;
And éyes, heárt, what looks, what lips yet gave you a
Rapturous love's greeting of realer, of rounder replies?

And the azurous hung hills are his world-wielding shoulder
Majestic – as a stallion stalwart, very-violet-sweet! –
These things, these things were here and but the beholder
Wanting; which two when they once meet,
The heart rears wings bold and bolder
And hurls for him, O half hurls earth for him off under his
                                                    feet.

D.H. LAWRENCE
(1885-1930)

Bavarian Gentians

NOT EVERY man has gentians in his house
in soft September, at slow, sad Michaelmas.

Bavarian gentians, big and dark,only dark
darkening the day-time, torch-like with the smoking blueness of
                                        Pluto's gloom,
ribbed and torch-like, with their blaze of darkness spread blue
down flattening into points, flattened under the sweep of white
                                        day
torch-flower of the blue-smoking darkness, Pluto's dark-blue
                                        daze,
black lamps from the halls of Dis, burning dark blue,
giving off darkness, blue darkness, as Demeter's pale lamps give
off light, lead me, then, lead the way.

Reach me a gentian, give me a torch!
let me guide myself with the blue, forked torch of this flower
down the darker and darker stairs, where blue is darkened on
                                        blueness
even where Persephone goes, just now, from the frosted
                                        September
to the sightless realm where darkness is awake upon the dark
and Persephone herself is but a voice
or a darkness invisible enfolded in the deeper dark
of the arms Plutonic, and pierced with the passion of dense
                                        gloom,
among the splendour of torches of darkness, shedding darkness
                    on the lost bride and her groom.

Moonrise

AND WHO has seen the moon, who has not seen
Her rise from out the chamber of the deep,
Flushed and grand and naked, as from the chamber
Of finished bridegroom, seen her rise and throw
Confession of delight upon the wave,
Littering the waves with her own superscription
Of bliss, till all her lambent beauty shakes towards us
Spread out and known at last, and we are sure
That beauty is a thing beyond the grave,
That perfect, bright experience never falls
To nothingness, and time will dim the moon
Sooner than our full consummation here
In this odd life will tarnish or pass away.

When the Ripe Fruit Falls

WHEN THE ripe fruit falls
its sweetness distils and trickles away into
the veins of the earth.

When fulfilled people die
the essential oil of their experience enters
the veins of living space, and adds a glisten
to the atom, to the body of immortal chaos.

For space is alive
and it stirs like a swan
whose feathers glisten
silky with oil of distilled experience.

GALLERY OF POETS

William Shakespeare

John Donne

Robert Herrick

George Herbert, 1674

Henry Vaughan

Thomas Phillips, William Blake

William Wordsworth, 1842, National Portrait Gallery, London

Samuel Taylor Coleridge

Percy Bysshe Shelley

Elizabeth Barrett Browning, by Macaire Havre,1859.

The Brontë sisters, by their brother Bramwell, c. 1834

Emily Dickinson

Thomas Hardy

D.H. Lawrence

A Note On Mystical Poetry in English

MYSTICAL EXPERIENCE is a difficult thing to define, as is 'mystical' poetry, or mysticism itself. A general definition is that mysticism lies at the core of religion. Mysticism is the set of beliefs, practices and ideas that grows up around the mystical experience. Religions are founded on mysticism. At the heart of Islam, for instance, is Sufism, the mystical dimension of Islamic religion. At the heart of Christianity are mystics such as St Paul, St Bernard of Clairvaux, Jacob Boehme, Hildegard of Bingen, St Catherine of Siena, and the passionate Spanish mystics, St John of the Cross and St Teresa. As I have selected from mystics or mystical works written originally in English, and not translations, this has precluded mystical writings by Plotinus, Heraclitus, Dante, Suso, Tauler, Boehme, Paracelsus, Hui-Neng, Chuang-tzu and any number of anonymous mystics from all over the world. A full-length anthology of mystical poetry would run to many volumes. Unfortunately, some mystics are not the best recorders of their experiences, which is partly why I have selected so many poets. It is not so much that some mystics do not create valuable accounts of their mystical experiences, it is rather that poets seem better able to put these feelings into words and stanzas.

I have taken a wide interpretation of mysticism and mystical poetry. I know some authorities contend that many types of poetry or religious feelings are not strictly 'mystical'. Many theologians and commentators on religion are protective about mystical experience, outlawing certain experiences.[1] Other critics of religion are more open-minded in their approach to mysticism, and include experiences such as hypnagogia, daydreaming, drug trances, hypnotism, orgasm, and other 'altered states of consciousness'.[2] For this selection, I have included works from poets not normally thought of as 'mystical' poets: Shakespeare, Hardy, and Brontë. Poets such as Vaughan, Herbert, Blake, Hopkins, Whitman and Donne are more typically artists that deliberately address religious or mystical experiences. The mystical aspects of the Metaphysical poets, for example, is well-known, and celebrated (Herbert, Vaughan, Crashaw, Traherne), and most of the Romantic poets wrote 'mystical' verse (Wordsworth most obviously – he is always cited in discussions on pantheism and Christian poetry – Keats, Shelley and Coleridge). Also included are writers that are definitely mystics: the great British mystics, such as Richard Rolle, Walter Hilton, Julian of Norwich and the author of *The Cloud of Unknowing*. There is no argument about the deep mystical feelings in these writers. Rolle is of course a poet, but including Julian of Norwich in an anthology of poetry requires some explanation. I have incorporated extracts of prose (from Julian of Norwich, Walter Hilton and Traherne, for example) because it seemed appropriate to include these mystics in a book of mystical work. Their prose is also 'poetic' (unlike other English mystics such as William Law). The mystical poetry here, then, takes in pantheism and Nature poetry (in Wordsworth, Whitman, Coleridge and Keats) as well the more orthodox Christian poetry (Donne, Crashaw, Traherne). Although most of the writers here are British, I have included some American writers: Longfellow, Emerson, Dickinson and Whitman. Walt Whitman is the grand master of pantheistic poetry, a truly abundant poet, one of the most prolix voices in poetry. He simply could not stop himself from writing like a flood. Many mystical poets are like this: the mystical experience ignites them, and sets the words flowing. Many mystics and mystical poets write long works, in order to circumscribe their experience (think of St John of the Cross, Meister Eckhart, Dante or Wordsworth). It's worth considering

Whitman further, because what applies to Whitman applies to many mystical poets, and because Whitman is in some ways the typical (as well the atypical) poet who's infused with mystical feelings. In Whitman, mystical tendencies are taken to extremes, but mystical poetry is *already* a poetry of extremes.3

There is magic, undoubtedly, in poetry, a mysticism or ecstasy that occurs when reading or hearing poetry. You experience good poetry with all five senses. No, with all six senses, with the magical, praeternatural sense awakened.4 Like art, poetry was originally part of magic and religion. At its best, poetry can still, even in a thoroughly secularized world, produce (or at least suggest) that thrill or even bliss that is part of mystical and magical experience. Although speaking of magic extends the definition of mysticism to include far too much ground for many theologians and religionists, they derive from similar sources and experiences. Not surprising, though, that most of the British and American poetry selected here revolves around the God of monotheism and Christianity. Even in works that derive from 'Classical' or 'pagan' themes (such as in Shelley or Shakespeare) Christianity is still a very strong presence (despite critics calling Shakespeare anti-Christian or 'pagan'). From the anonymous *Cloud of Unknowing* and *Quia Amore Langueo* through George Herbert and the Metaphysical poets to Emily Brontë and Thomas Hardy, Christianity infuses every aspect of the mystical experience. No surprise, this, as Judaeo-Christianity is the religion of the West. Modern poets such as D.H. Lawrence (who ends this anthology) have shown just how powerful Christian symbols and images can still be in a secular age. Lawrence showed that mystical poetry is by no means destroyed by world wars or mass secularization.

Notes

1. For example, R.C. Zaehner, William Johnston, Paul Tillich, Karl Barth and Bernard Lonegran.

2. For example, Aldous Huxley, Alan Watts, Willard Johnson, Joseph Campbell, Mircea Eliade and C.G. Jung.

3. David Daiches, discussing A.E. Housman's definition that good poetry makes the hair stand up writes: 'there are moments in our reading of poetry when we experience that special kind of *frisson* that tells us we are engaging with an expression of some uniquely revelatory insight into some aspect of experience.' (David Daiches: *God and the Poets: The Gifford Lectures, 1983*, Clarendon Press, Oxford, 1984, 218)

4. Discussing Whitman's *Song of Myself*, David Daiches writes: 'the tone here is direct, familiar, even slangy. And the poem is *addressed* to a reader, addressed with studied negligence... for all its apparent ego-centricity the poem is not focused on the poet's own self and his own mood, as so much English nineteenth-century poetry is; it takes real cognizance of other people and other things... The language here is completely free of the brooding introspection cadence, that sense of reducing all light to twilight or starlight or moonlight, the transcendental hush of lonely genius communing with itself, that is so common in Victorian poetry. Whitman's poetic self is both separate and isolated *and* participating, part of a community, 'both in and out of the game and watching and wondering at it'. The self observes, half humorously, a little wryly, the self observing.' (Daiches, ib., 98-99)

Beauties, Beasts, and Enchantment

CLASSIC FRENCH FAIRY TALES

Translated and with an Introduction
by Jack Zipes

A collection of 36 classic French fairy tales translated by renowned writer Jack Zipes.
Cinderella, Beauty and the Beast, Sleeping Beauty and *Little Red Riding Hood* are among the
classic fairy tales in this amazing book.
Includes illustrations from fairy tale collections.
Jack Zipes has written and published widely on fairy tales.

'Terrific... a succulent array of 17th and 18th century 'salon' fairy tales'
- The New York Times Book Review

'These tales are adventurous, thrilling in a way fairy tales are meant to be... The translation
from the French is modern, happily free of archaic and hyperbolic language... a fine and
sophisticated collection' *- New York Tribune*

'Enjoyable to read... a unique collection of French regional folklore' *- Library Journal*

'Charming stories accompanied by attractive pen-and-ink drawings' *- Chattanooga Times*

Introduction and illustrations   612pp.   ISBN 9781861712510 Pbk   ISBN 9781861713193 Hbk

Life, Life
Selected Poems

Arseny Tarkovsky

translated and edited by Virginia Rounding

Arseny Tarkovsky is the neglected Russian poet, father of the acclaimed film director Andrei Tarkovsky. This new book gathers together many of Tarkovsky's most lyrical and heartfelt poems, in Rounding's clear, new translations. Many of Tarkovsky's poems appeared in his son's films, such as *Mirror, Stalker, Nostalghia and The Sacrifice*. There is an introduction by Rounding, and a bibliography of both Arseny and Andrei Tarkovsky.

Bibliography and notes 124pp 3rd ed ISBN 9781861712660 Hbk ISBN 9781861711144

MAURICE SENDAK

& the art of children's book illustration

L.M. Poole

Maurice Sendak is the widely acclaimed American children's book author and illustrator. This critical study focuses on his famous trilogy, *Where the Wild Things Are*, *In the Night Kitchen* and *Outside Over There*, as well as the early works and Sendak's superb depictions of the Grimm Brothers' fairy tales in *The Juniper Tree*. L.M. Poole begins with a chapter on children's book illustration, in particular the treatment of fairy tales. Sendak's work is situated within the history of children's book illustration, and he is compared with many contemporary authors.

Fully illustrated. The book has been revised and updated for this edition.
ISBN 9781861714282 Pbk   ISBN 9781861713469 Hbk

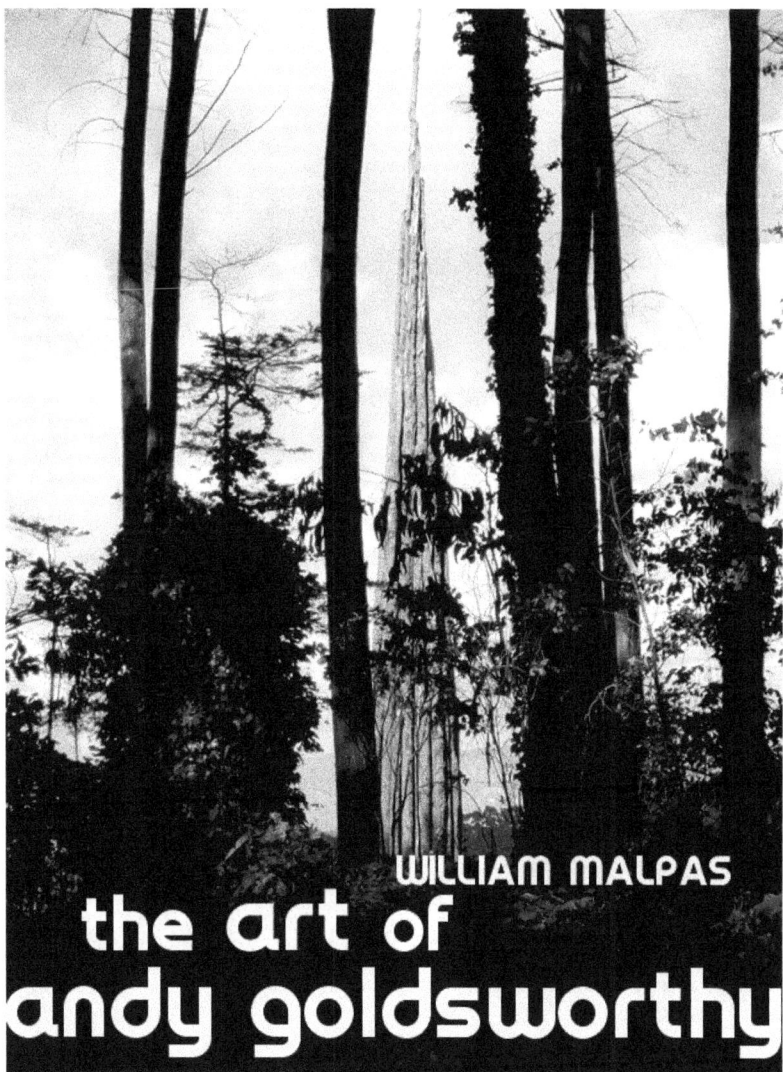

This is the most comprehensive and detailed account of the art of Andy Goldsworthy available.

This study of Andy Goldsworthy discusses all of Goldsworthy's major exhibitions, books and projects, including the *Sheepfolds* project; *Garden of Stones* in New York; TV and dance collaborations; and the books *Wood*, *Stone*, *Time* and *Passage*. William Malpas surveys all of Goldsworthy's output, and analyzes his relation with other land artists such as Robert Smithson, the Christos, Walter de Maria, Chris Drury, Richard Long and David Nash; women sculptors; sculpture in the modern era; and Goldsworthy's place in the contemporary British art scene.

The book has been updated and revised for this new edition.

ISBN 9781861714107 Pbk   ISBN 9781861714114 Hbk
Fully illustrated   www.crmoon.com

CRESCENT MOON PUBLISHING

web: www.crmoon.com e-mail: cresmopub@yahoo.co.uk

ARTS, PAINTING, SCULPTURE

The Art of Andy Goldsworthy
Andy Goldsworthy: Touching Nature
Andy Goldsworthy in Close-Up
Andy Goldsworthy: Pocket Guide
Andy Goldsworthy In America
Land Art: A Complete Guide
The Art of Richard Long
Richard Long: Pocket Guide
Land Art In the UK
Land Art in Close-Up
Land Art In the U.S.A.
Land Art: Pocket Guide
Installation Art in Close-Up
Minimal Art and Artists In the 1960s and After
Colourfield Painting
Land Art DVD, TV documentary
Andy Goldsworthy DVD, TV documentary
The Erotic Object: Sexuality in Sculpture From Prehistory to the Present Day
Sex in Art: Pornography and Pleasure in Painting and Sculpture
Postwar Art
Sacred Gardens: The Garden in Myth, Religion and Art
Glorification: Religious Abstraction in Renaissance and 20th Century Art
Early Netherlandish Painting
Leonardo da Vinci
Piero della Francesca
Giovanni Bellini
Fra Angelico: Art and Religion in the Renaissance
Mark Rothko: The Art of Transcendence
Frank Stella: American Abstract Artist
Jasper Johns
Brice Marden
Alison Wilding: The Embrace of Sculpture
Vincent van Gogh: Visionary Landscapes
Eric Gill: Nuptials of God
Constantin Brancusi: Sculpting the Essence of Things
Max Beckmann
Caravaggio
Gustave Moreau
Egon Schiele: Sex and Death In Purple Stockings
Delizioso Fotografico Fervore: Works In Process 1
Sacro Cuore: Works In Process 2
The Light Eternal: J.M.W. Turner
The Madonna Glorified: Karen Arthurs

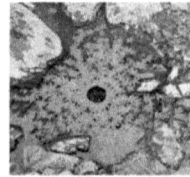

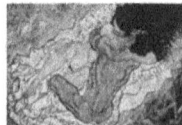

LITERATURE

J.R.R. Tolkien: The Books, The Films, The Whole Cultural Phenomenon
J.R.R. Tolkien: Pocket Guide
Tolkien's Heroic Quest
The *Earthsea* Books of Ursula Le Guin
Beauties, Beasts and Enchantment: Classic French Fairy Tales
German Popular Stories by the Brothers Grimm
Philip Pullman and *His Dark Materials*
Sexing Hardy: Thomas Hardy and Feminism
Thomas Hardy's *Tess of the d'Urbervilles*

Thomas Hardy's *Jude the Obscure*
Thomas Hardy: The Tragic Novels
Love and Tragedy: Thomas Hardy
The Poetry of Landscape in Hardy
Wessex Revisited: Thomas Hardy and John Cowper Powys
Wolfgang Iser: Essays and Interviews

Petrarch, Dante and the Troubadours
Maurice Sendak and the Art of Children's Book Illustration
Andrea Dworkin

Cixous, Irigaray, Kristeva: The *Jouissance* of French Feminism
Julia Kristeva: Art, Love, Melancholy, Philosophy, Semiotics and Psychoanalysis
Hélène Cixous I Love You: The *Jouissance* of Writing
Luce Irigaray: Lips, Kissing, and the Politics of Sexual Difference
Peter Redgrove: Here Comes the Flood
Peter Redgrove: Sex-Magic-Poetry-Cornwall
Lawrence Durrell: Between Love and Death, East and West
Love, Culture & Poetry: Lawrence Durrell

Cavafy: Anatomy of a Soul
German Romantic Poetry: Goethe, Novalis, Heine, Hölderlin
Feminism and Shakespeare
Shakespeare: Love, Poetry & Magic

The Passion of D.H. Lawrence
D.H. Lawrence: Symbolic Landscapes
D.H. Lawrence: Infinite Sensual Violence
Rimbaud: Arthur Rimbaud and the Magic of Poetry
The Ecstasies of John Cowper Powys
Sensualism and Mythology: The Wessex Novels of John Cowper Powys
Amorous Life: John Cowper Powys and the Manifestation of Affectivity (H.W. Fawkner)
Postmodern Powys: New Essays on John Cowper Powys (Joe Boulter)
Rethinking Powys: Critical Essays on John Cowper Powys
Paul Bowles & Bernardo Bertolucci
Rainer Maria Rilke
Joseph Conrad: *Heart of Darkness*
In the Dim Void: Samuel Beckett
Samuel Beckett Goes into the Silence

André Gide: Fiction and Fervour
Jackie Collins and the Blockbuster Novel
Blinded By Her Light: The Love-Poetry of Robert Graves
The Passion of Colours: Travels In Mediterranean Lands
Poetic Forms

POETRY

Ursula Le Guin: Walking In Cornwall
Peter Redgrove: Here Comes The Flood
Peter Redgrove: Sex-Magic-Poetry-Cornwall
Dante: Selections From the Vita Nuova
Petrarch, Dante and the Troubadours
William Shakespeare: Sonnets
William Shakespeare: Complete Poems
Blinded By Her Light: The Love-Poetry of Robert Graves
Emily Dickinson: Selected Poems
Emily Brontë: Poems
Thomas Hardy: Selected Poems
Percy Bysshe Shelley: Poems
John Keats: Selected Poems
Joh n Keats: Poems of 1820
D.H. Lawrence: Selected Poems
Edmund Spenser: Poems
Edmund Spenser: Amoretti
John Donne: Poems
Henry Vaughan: Poems
Sir Thomas Wyatt: Poems
Robert Herrick: Selected Poems
Rilke: Space, Essence and Angels in the Poetry of Rainer Maria Rilke
Rainer Maria Rilke: Selected Poems
Friedrich Hölderlin: Selected Poems
Arseny Tarkovsky: Selected Poems
Arthur Rimbaud: Selected Poems
Arthur Rimbaud: A Season in Hell
Arthur Rimbaud and the Magic of Poetry
Novalis: Hymns To the Night
German Romantic Poetry
Paul Verlaine: Selected Poems
Elizaethan Sonnet Cycles
D.J. Enright: By-Blows
Jeremy Reed: Brigitte's Blue Heart
Jeremy Reed: Claudia Schiffer's Red Shoes
Gorgeous Little Orpheus
Radiance: New Poems
Crescent Moon Book of Nature Poetry
Crescent Moon Book of Love Poetry
Crescent Moon Book of Mystical Poetry
Crescent Moon Book of Elizabethan Love Poetry
Crescent Moon Book of Metaphysical Poetry
Crescent Moon Book of Romantic Poetry
Pagan America: New American Poetry

MEDIA, CINEMA, FEMINISM and CULTURAL STUDIES

J.R.R. Tolkien: The Books, The Films, The Whole Cultural Phenomenon
J.R.R. Tolkien: Pocket Guide
The *Lord of the Rings* Movies: Pocket Guide
The Cinema of Hayao Miyazaki
Hayao Miyazaki: *Princess Mononoke*: Pocket Movie Guide
Hayao Miyazaki: *Spirited Away*: Pocket Movie Guide
Tim Burton : Hallowe'en For Hollywood
Ken Russell
Ken Russell: *Tommy*: Pocket Movie Guide
The Ghost Dance: The Origins of Religion
The Peyote Cult
Cixous, Irigaray, Kristeva: The *Jouissance* of French Feminism
Julia Kristeva: Art, Love, Melancholy, Philosophy, Semiotics and Psychoanalysis
Luce Irigaray: Lips, Kissing, and the Politics of Sexual Difference
Hélene Cixous I Love You: The *Jouissance* of Writing
Andrea Dworkin
'Cosmo Woman': The World of Women's Magazines
Women in Pop Music
HomeGround: The Kate Bush Anthology
Discovering the Goddess (Geoffrey Ashe)
The Poetry of Cinema
The Sacred Cinema of Andrei Tarkovsky
Andrei Tarkovsky: Pocket Guide
Andrei Tarkovsky: *Mirror*: Pocket Movie Guide
Andrei Tarkovsky: *The Sacrifice*: Pocket Movie Guide
Walerian Borowczyk: Cinema of Erotic Dreams
Jean-Luc Godard: The Passion of Cinema
Jean-Luc Godard: *Hail Mary*: Pocket Movie Guide
Jean-Luc Godard: *Contempt*: Pocket Movie Guide
Jean-Luc Godard: *Pierrot le Fou*: Pocket Movie Guide
John Hughes and Eighties Cinema
Ferris Bueller's Day Off: Pocket Movie Guide
Jean-Luc Godard: Pocket Guide
The Cinema of Richard Linklater
Liv Tyler: Star In Ascendance
Blade Runner and the Films of Philip K. Dick
Paul Bowles and Bernardo Bertolucci
Media Hell: Radio, TV and the Press
An Open Letter to the BBC
Detonation Britain: Nuclear War in the UK
Feminism and Shakespeare
Wild Zones: Pornography, Art and Feminism
Sex in Art: Pornography and Pleasure in Painting and Sculpture
Sexing Hardy: Thomas Hardy and Feminism

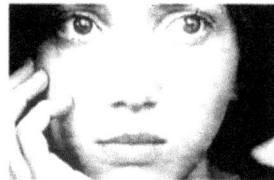

The Light Eternal is a model monograph, an exemplary job. The subject matter of the book is beautifully organised and dead on beam. (Lawrence Durrell)
It is amazing for me to see my work treated with such passion and respect. (Andrea Dworkin)

CRESCENT MOON PUBLISHING
P.O. Box 1312, Maidstone, Kent, ME14 5XU, Great Britain. www.crmoon.com

cresmopub@yahoo.co.uk   www.crescentmoon.org.uk

www.ingramcontent.com/pod-product-compliance
Lightning Source LLC
Chambersburg PA
CBHW060209070426
42447CB00035B/2867